A QUIET PLACE IN A CRAZY WORLD

JONI EARECKSON TADA

A QUIET PLACE IN A CRAZY WORLD

*Drawing
Near to God
Through
Prayer & Praise*

MULTNOMAH BOOKS

A Quiet Place in a Crazy World

published by Multnomah Books
a part of the Questar publishing family

© 1993 by Joni Eareckson Tada

International Standard Book Number: 0-88070606-6

Cover design by David Uttley
Edited by Larry R. Libby

Printed in the United States of America

94 95 96 97 98 99 00 01 — 10 9 8 7 6 5 4 3

TO

MARY LANCE SISK AND BUNNY WARLEN

Mary Lance—When I asked God,
"Teach me how to pray," He sent...you.
As my prayer mentor,
you have shown me that prayer
is intimacy with God;
and
Bunny—What a fool for Christ you are,
believing that prayer is no work at all,
but a joy! And what joy you must give
the Father when you pray.

ACKNOWLEDGEMENTS

Unforgettable thoughts should never be forgotten.

When I looked back over the manuscript for this book, I recognized timeless stories and insights from some of my favorite friends and authors. You, too, will notice that Charles H. Spurgeon through his unforgettable sermons inspired much of the content. If I had been around in his day, I would have sat in the front row of his church every Sunday. For this reason, I must thank Baker Book House for "letting Spurgeon live" through publishing his *Twelve Sermons on Prayer*. I'm grateful to Zondervan Publishing House and Steve Estes—the insights shared in *A Step Further* are still having an impact for the Lord Jesus as new and different readers enjoy this book.

Readers who are familiar with my work may also recognize some thoughts from my earlier book, *Secret Strength*.

Thanks to my friends at Questar for rescuing this manuscript which originally appeared as *Seeking God: My Journey of Prayer and Praise*. Had it not been for them, *Seeking God* would have been lost in the crush of various publishing acquisitions. I'm grateful to Questar for helping me expand and reissue the content under this new title.

Finally, I'm grateful to Bev Singleton, Larry Libby, and Shari MacDonald for helping to give shape to my words and, ultimately, to people's prayers.

CONTENTS

A QUIET PLACE

God meets us in *places*.

Have you ever thought about it? He has made us as a people who live in time and space. And if He is going to meet with us at all, this eternal, all-powerful, everywhere-present God must condescend to meet with us at a certain location, at a certain time.

The mighty Creator of the universe must bind Himself to a penciled line in my date book.

And the wonder of it is, He does! Down through the centuries, He always has.

He strolled with Adam through the Garden in the cool of the day.

He wrestled with Jacob through a long night by a stream called Jabbok.

He comforted the fugitive David in a dank limestone cave called Adullum.

He stood with a grief-torn mom and dad in an upstairs room, by the bed of their dead (but soon to be alive!) daughter.

He crossed paths with His disciples in the middle of the night, in the middle of the sea, in the middle of a storm.

He meets us ANYPLACE.

There is never a place where He is not. He waits in every room we're about to enter. He stands quietly in the back of every elevator—up or down—before we step through the doors. He lingers around every bend of every path we will ever walk. He's in the dark kitchen when we get up at night for a glass of milk. He's in the recovery room when we come out from under anesthetic. On a long dirt road, He's under the tree in the field where we pause to rest. There is no place too remote, no night too black, no cave too deep, no mountain peak too high for the immediate, awesome, pervasive, loving presence of the Lord our God.

Yes, He meets with us ANYPLACE. But He also meets with us SOMEPLACE.

Somebody once said, "I can pray *every*where *all* the time, because I can pray *some*where *some* of the time." There is a special, specific place of meeting with God, which is as the bedroom to the bride and bridegroom. A chamber of hallowedness and holiness. A familiar place where we've met Him again and again. Whether it's kneeling at the bedside of our Sealy Posture-Pedic or it's in the driver's seat on our commute, or at the railing of our sleeping child's crib…there is a habitual "someplace" of meeting God that is more sacred and special to us than a myriad "anyplaces."

For me, that place is my bedroom.

That's the one little spot on this spinning planet where I always meet God. As soon as I wheel into my bedroom and see the side lamp lit, the bed covers pulled back just so, and my turn-at-night pillows on the chair, it all signals a Pavlovian response in my mind. *It's time to pray.* This isn't just the place where I get eight hours of sleep, this is where God meets me.

We all need such places. We need hallowed chambers in the rambling structures of our lives. In developing that discipline of always meeting God some place, some of the time, we begin to see how He opens up meeting places where we encounter Him everywhere, all of the time. "Pray without ceasing" becomes a way of looking at every place as a point of encountering the Lord. A holy intersection.

When I was a little girl, I visited my Uncle Vincent's house on the eastern shore, near Easton, Maryland. One afternoon Uncle Vince (he was actually an older cousin) took me upstairs to show me his "prayer room."

I remember thinking, *This is strange. This is a little rigid. God ought to be meeting Uncle Vince on the golf course, like He meets me when I go horseback riding, or when I go hiking with Daddy. How odd that Uncle Vince needs this little room.*

Uncle Vince's sacred cubicle was not to my taste. He had found some stained glass from an old church in Easton, and had made tall, vertical windows. He had hung a couple of old, musty tapestries on the fake paneling. There was a little prayer kneeler, and an open Bible on a stand.

It seemed so odd to me. Stuffy. Tacky. I wasn't drawn to it at all. But in later years, looking back, I found myself thinking, *How wise of Uncle Vince to have had a place all those years where he met Jesus.* That's probably the reason why he *could* pray on the golf course and when he went hiking with us. Uncle Vince encountered God every place…because he had one place.

How we need such a place, a quiet place…

...In A Crazy World

This *is* a crazy world.

Like that no-wax floor of yours that always needs waxing...the rust-proof pipes under your sink that turn red-orange in less than a year...the never-need-repair top-brand washing machine whose engine belt keeps breaking.

It's crazy.

TV advertisements for *Self* magazine and Playtex bras bookend a story of massacres in Bosnia. A handicapped infant left to starve to death in a neo-natal unit while a couple two thousand miles away search high and low to adopt a child—any child. Millions of dollars are spent to protect the eggs of birds on an endangered species list while human babies are aborted in the third trimester. Battered wives paste on smiles as they dress for church. A preteen girl writes in her prayer diary, "My daddy took away my innocence last night."

It's all crazy.

I've seen the insanity and cruelty of man in places such as Bucharest, Manila, Quito,...Auschwitz.

It began in Eden, when man and woman chose to part company with their Creator. Whenever man gains control, chaos and darkness reign. It is an insanity that blights beauty, shatters peace, and brings hurt and injustice and cruelty and neglect. It is an insanity that preys upon the innocent and crushes dreams and quenches the light of hope in young eyes.

But this is still "my Father's world."

> He shines in all that's fair,
> in the rustling grass
> I hear Him pass
> He speaks to me everywhere.

In His coming, the Lord Jesus hallowed this broken, crazy world. He breathed earth's air and felt the warmth of its sun and drank its cool water and walked its dusty highways. Earth's soil drank in drops of divine sweat and tears and blood.

The Holy Spirit is here, the wise and gentle Counselor. He speaks through His Word, He shines through the lives of countless believers all over the world.

It is a crazy world.

We keep crazy schedules.

Life speeds by at a blur.

The crazy waves of circumstances roll over us, overwhelm us, threaten to drag us under.

Yet God is with us…no matter where we find ourselves in life. Right in the middle of the craziness. And anywhere, at any time, we may turn to Him. Walk with Him. Talk to Him. Hear His voice. Feel His hand. And catch—even if just for a moment—the fragrance of heaven.

It's an island of sanity in a sea of confusion.

It's a quiet place.

And it is ours.

Whenever we look up into the face of our Father,
    whenever we reach for His hand
        whenever we quiet our spirit to hear His voice
        we have found a place of refuge
            this crazy world can never take away.

Joni Eareckson Tada
Agoura Hills, California

CHAPTER ONE

A PLACE OF SEEKING

But if...you seek the LORD your God,
you will find him if you look for him
with all your heart and with all your soul
(Deuteronomy 4:29).

I t was a clear, cool autumn night. The camp meeting hall was in the motel conference center up the road from an ancient natural bridge formation. I sat in a metal folding chair in the back of the dim, old structure, listening to a speaker talk about God's love and provision. He was describing the gospel, but his launch point was the Ten Commandments.

PLACE:
Young Life High
School Retreat,
Natural Bridge,
Virginia
TIME:
November 1964

I'll never forget his challenge. "Kids, what I want you to do is measure your own life up against each of these commandments as I talk about them."

Some of it went over my head. I didn't know what "bear false witness" meant, and I wasn't married, so I hadn't committed adultery. But I knew enough to know that my life was falling short.

Rather than being driven to my knees in repentance, however, I became angry. How unfair of God to give us a bunch of rules and laws we couldn't keep! Draping my sweatshirt over my shoulders, I walked out of the meeting. I remember thinking, *This is ridiculous. I can't keep those commandments. Nobody can!*

I exited the musty-smelling hall into a brisk autumn night, resplendent with stars. Climbing the dark path that wound up the hillside toward the cabins, I found a big flat rock in a clearing and plunked myself down.

Leaning back, I looked up through dark, towering pine trees into the vast, starry dome. I remember trying to puzzle it all through. It was a conscious effort to really get to the bottom of this gospel thing. *Now what is this seeking God stuff all about? How does this all fit? He gives us commands He knows we can't keep. Yet He expects perfection! Jesus came, and because He was God, He did keep all the commands. He did live a perfect life. And then, at the end, they took Him and—Whoa! Of course!*

It was as if the proverbial light bulb lit up over my head. *Yes! That's what the cross was all about! That's why He had to die!*

God reached down to me in that place—on a rock, under the stars—and touched my mind. The puzzle pieces suddenly came together and I understood my need of a Savior. He met me in my place of seeking.

A little less than three years later, He met me again. In another place of seeking. Only this second encounter was less like solving a mental puzzle. It was more like clutching a single rope dangling over a bottomless pit.

It's tough being a teenager. It's even tougher when you're seventeen and facing life in a wheelchair.

I receive a lot of letters from thirteen-, fourteen-, and fifteen-year-olds, and many of them honestly feel they should end it all. They simply can't face the fact that an injury has paralyzed their legs or an accident has taken away their sight.

Even though many years have passed since I was that age, all those feelings and memories are as fresh as if they happened yesterday. Maybe that's because "life on my feet" stopped when I was seventeen, when I broke my neck in a diving accident.

PLACE:
*University of
Maryland Hospital*
TIME:
October 1967

The toughest part of those early days in the hospital was living up to my reputation as a Christian when people came to visit me. I felt like people expected me to put on a happy face. Try as I might, I just couldn't. My failure made me feel even more guilty about letting down my parents, my pastor, and my Christian friends. Being newly injured, I suddenly realized there was a lot more to all those Bible verses I had learned in Sunday school. Romans 8:28, "all things work together for good" (KJV), had always served me well when I was on my feet. Of course, my toughest problem in those days was sweating out fifty sit-ups in gym class or arguing with my sister after she borrowed my clothes. Hardship meant staying up late to cram for an algebra test.

Would all those Sunday school verses work now that I had to sit in a wheelchair? I wasn't so sure. In that hospital, I felt like I had been hit with a sudden dose of "growing up," and I didn't like it one bit.

But one night, lying face down on my Stryker frame in the dark, after everyone else had gone home, I plunged to my lowest ebb. For days I had begged my friends to help me commit suicide,

A Place of Seeking

but they wouldn't do it. I had pleaded for their mothers' sleeping pills or their fathers' razor blades, but they wouldn't bring them. I was so helpless I couldn't even kill myself!

I wanted so much to die, but God wouldn't let me die. So I had to live—but how could I live? From the numb blackness of my despair, I suddenly found myself praying, *God, if I can't die, show me how to live, please!* It was short, to the point, but it was a prayer voiced straight from the deep-down soul of me.

As a fourteen-year-old on that rock in Natural Bridge, Virginia, I somehow imagined that I was bringing something to God by responding to Him. *Here I am, God, aren't You lucky?* As if I was doing Him some kind of great favor by opening my life to His mercy.

But in the hospital, face down in the Stryker frame, in the middle of the night, I knew I had *nothing* to bring Him. Nothing at all.

Things didn't change overnight, but with that simple prayer my outlook began to change. I realized that "growing up" was just something I was going to have to learn how to do. I would have to learn how to do the impossible—handle life in a wheelchair.

Your place of seeking may be very different than mine. Chances are, you aren't at this moment lying face down in a hospital Stryker frame. But your struggles are just as real. You might not have the strength to say much more to God than a simple prayer like "show me how to live." But God is not looking for a lot of fancy words. He can take that simple desire of your heart and help you find strength and refuge through the power of prayer.

A Quiet Place in a Crazy World

Psalm 34:18 says, "The LORD is close to the brokenhearted and saves those who are crushed in spirit." You may not change overnight with such a simple prayer, but right now you can ask God to show you how to live. Pray it and mean it. And then watch your outlook change. You just might start living the impossible.

PRAYER MOVES GOD

It's been said faith may move mountains, but prayer moves God. Amazing, isn't it, that our prayers, whether grand and glorious or feeble and faint, can move the very heart of God who created the universe? To walk with God we must make it a practice to talk with God, and that's what this book is all about: finding a quiet place—physically and spiritually—where you can meet and *commune* with God in the midst of your sometimes crazy world.

Prayer moves God, and when God moves in your life, things get exciting! Years ago I never dreamed that God would move in my life the way He has. Even after my accident, when I signed up at the University of Maryland for art and English classes, I never realized how God would use diverse elements in my life to mold me to His will. But I sensed God was preparing me for something. He began meeting me in a quiet place in my room, a quiet place in my heart where we still meet today. You, too, have a quiet place where you can meet with God, whether you have discovered it yet or not. It is there that you can find refuge from life's storms; there that you will find peace in the midst of all the craziness; there that you will discover the power of prayer.

I'm not perfect; I'm still learning about prayer. God is still revealing His plan for me, and He and I are still in this adventure of life together. But I've learned a few lessons I'd like to share with you in the hopes that your prayer life will become richer.

THE IMPORTANCE OF PRAYER

I am a good visual aid to illustrate how important a healthy prayer life is. My mind has some great ideas for my hands and legs to carry out, but there has been a break in the communication system—my hands and legs just can't carry out what my mind asks them to do. Colossians 2:19 describes men who have "lost connection with the Head, from whom the whole body, supported and held together by its ligaments and sinews, grows as God causes it to grow."

A healthy spiritual body of believers should take their direction from Christ, their Head, just as individual Christians should maintain the communication system with Christ. Without communication with our Head, Jesus Christ, we grow ineffective and our spiritual muscles atrophy.

Prayer is the hub of that communication. Prayer is the pause that empowers. It is the one weapon our enemy, the Devil, cannot duplicate or counterfeit. It is not measured by its length but by its depth. Effective prayer doesn't require a Ph.D.—it only requires a willingness to share your thoughts with God. A willingness to let Him share His thoughts with you.

HOLDING ON TO TRUTH

One of the wonderful things about prayer is that it gives you something to depend on...something to cling to.

Have you ever held on to something as though your life

depended on it? I have. When I was four years old, I used to go horseback riding with my family. I'm not talking about sitting on some small pony being led around a little ring. I'm talking about wild and woolly, galloping jaunts up and down hills and through pastures, jumping fences, and splashing through streams. Real horseback riding.

At four, I was too young to have my own horse, and I'm not sure a pony fit for a four-year-old could have kept up with my father and sisters, anyway. So when we went horseback riding, I sat behind my father on his big horse. With my tiny hands, I'd hang on to his belt for dear life, and off we'd go! I'd bounce up and down on the back of his saddle, sliding this way and that, but as long as I had a strong hold on that belt, I knew I was safe.

That memory came back to me recently when I was reading Ephesians 6, that portion of Scripture where Paul talks about the armor of God. Paul tells us to put on the breastplate of righteousness and the helmet of salvation and take up the sword of the Spirit.

Paul mentions a very important part of the armor in verse 14: "Stand firm then, with the *belt of truth* buckled around your waist." The belt of truth, especially in prayer, is like a foundation. We put it on before we put on other things, and if there's anything we ought not lose grip on, it should be the belt of truth. The Bible says we are to approach God "in spirit and in truth" (John 4:24).

Another way of putting that?

Approach God in prayer with heartfelt honesty.

Now I'm not much different from when I was a child. When the going gets rough and I feel I'm being led up and down, this way and that, I know I have got that belt. There are truths about God that I can hold on to.

God is in control.

He leads me along a path He has planned.

Nothing can touch me that is not in His plan.

He's passionate about my highest good.

His grace, available and abundant, more than sustains.

The craziness will pass. He will lead me through. An end is in sight.

These are the strands that weave the belt of truth, and I know that as long as I hang on, I will be safe. My world won't seem as crazy. That's the incredible power of prayer.

Job had a firm grip on the belt of truth, and his story has always been an inspiration to me. Some people say the book of Job is about his crazy world of suffering. Others say it's a story of faith or the sovereignty of God or the relationship between God and the Devil, but I think the book of Job is about prayer. Consider Job's cry:

PLACE:
The home of Job in
the Land of Uz

TIME:
In the days of the
patriarchs

If only I knew where to find him; if only I could go to his dwelling! I would state my case before him and fill my mouth with arguments. I would find out what he would answer me, and consider what he would say (Job 23:3-5).

You know the story of Job. He was an upright and righteous man, a man blessed of God. He had seven sons and three daughters, and he owned seven thousand sheep, three thousand camels, five hundred oxen, five hundred donkeys, and had a large number of servants. He was, the Bible tells us, "the greatest man among all the people of the East" (Job 1:3).

Job was a godly father to his children, a humble man before his neighbors, and a priest to his large household. But then Satan took aim at Job.

Job was feeling as though he were the target in a cosmic game of darts between God and the Devil. His property was either ruined or stolen, and his family killed. He was covered with boils, and he sat in a big pile of ashes, surrounded by critical friends and a nagging wife. He had a lot to talk to God about.

JOB'S RIGHT REACTION

Job's friends gathered around for seven days of silent sympathy, then they began prying. "Come on, Job," they said. "Surely you've done something terribly wrong and this is God's discipline. Fess up, and tell us all about it."

Then Job prayed. But listen to his prayer—he didn't pray, "Oh, that I might be healed of these boils," or "Oh, that I might have my children back," or even, "Oh, that these friends and my wife would get off my back!" Instead, Job's desire was to see the Father's face and to feel His smile. He expressed his longings in the twenty-third chapter, saying, "If only I knew where to find him! I would state my case before him...and consider what he would say."

This may seem off the subject, but think: What do you get when you squeeze an orange? Orange juice? Maybe, if no one has tampered with the orange or already squeezed it. When you squeeze an orange, what comes out is whatever is inside!

What happens when life "squeezes" a Christian? What is revealed is whatever is inside. A hypocrite, or someone who simply pretends to be a child of God, resents affliction and runs when troubled times come. His cowardice and pretense come out.

A self-centered Christian may complain for a while, but, in time, affliction can bring him to his knees. Then his heart can be drained of the selfishness and resentment, making him better able to approach God as a child would seek his father.

Some Christians treat God as a kind of insurance agent. In hard times, they expect Him to issue a claim check to restore what they've lost. While waiting for Him to change their circumstances for the better, they withhold fellowship from Him. Life's "squeeze" reveals their lack of submission and stubborn attitudes.

It is the heaven-born instinct of a child of God to seek a place of shelter beneath the wings of the Almighty. The tendency to complain or to assert that God owes us something is not spiritual. When the world of a child of God cracks apart, the godly instinct is to say with Job, "Oh, that I might find Him."

Job longed for God's presence. God had not left him, nor had He stopped protecting His child, but Job felt as though he had lost the smile of God: "Oh, that I knew where to find Him!"

Have you ever responded the way Job did? Yes, you've been obedient. No, you haven't run in the other direction. And you haven't been self-centered or demanded an explanation from God before you agree to worship Him. But you long for His smile. You wish to see His face in the stormy clouds. Your heart aches as you cry, "Oh, that I might find Him!"

That was Job's heartache. Even in despair and distress, the

desire of Job's heart was to seek God. And, oh, what a prepared heart for prayer he had. Why? Because he did not lose his grip on those things about God he knew to be true. And it was that Almighty God and the truth of His Word that was the desire of Job's heart.

What a way to begin your spiritual journey of prayer and praise: Desire God.

YOUR QUIET PLACE...

Prayer is what communication with God is all about. And what does He require as we approach Him in prayer? Truth. Genuineness. Sincerity. Heartfelt honesty. And please know this to be true of God: When we call on Him in truth, He listens! There's only one reaction you could have toward love so great. In fact, why don't you make it your prayer right now?

Oh Lord, if I were to be wholeheartedly honest with You right now, I'd have to admit I've often run in the other direction when trials squeeze me. At times, I've been a first-class hypocrite. But, like Job, I want to find You. I want to feel Your smile. Help me make that my heart's desire, in Jesus' name.

Congratulations. You're on your way. Your heart is now prepared to meet with God in prayer.

CHAPTER TWO

A PLACE OF REFUGE

—

He who dwells in the shelter of the Most High
will rest in the shadow of the Almighty.
I will say of the LORD, "He is my refuge and my fortress,
my God, in whom I trust"
(Psalm 91:1-2).

C an beauty be terrifying? If you don't feel a little tremor running up and down your back on a clear morning on Lake George, you'd better check your pulse.

The sun crests Crystal Crag, spilling into a dark, bright, blue sky. A ghost moon, tissue thin, clings to the horizon. In the clear, pristine air, shadows seem chiseled and black, with knife edges. Sounds carry an impossible distance: the clunk of oars in the oarlocks of a faraway rowboat; the murmur of two fisherman on a distant shore; the gentle lap of waves against the side of the boat. Underneath it all, a deep, pervasive roaring, more felt than heard, of wind sweeping a thousand cliffs.

PLACE:
In a Rowboat
on Mammoth Lakes,
California
TIME:
August 1981

Lake George itself is a massive bowl of clear, glacial turquoise on the backbone of a mighty mountain range. When the morning sunlight shoots through its crystal depths, bits of mica on the lake bottom fire it back in tiny, crystalline explosions.

I draw my lungs full of air—so cold it stings—and throw back my head to gaze at the overpowering castle-like spires of Crystal Crag. What I feel next can only be described as vertigo—as if the mountain—somehow top-heavy—is going to fall on me.

Did David feel that same vertigo, that same dizzy rush and queasiness in the pit of his stomach when he wrote these words?

O LORD, our Lord,
how majestic is your name in all the earth!
You have set your glory above the heavens.
When I consider your heavens,
the work of your fingers,
the moon and the stars,
which you have set in place,
what is man that you are mindful of him,
the son of man that you care for him?
(Psalm 8:1,3-4).

David was blown away in the jet-blast of God's beauty and greatness and power. He found himself shaking his head, saying, "What? *What?* What is puny man that You take thought of Him?"

He could have felt squashed, overwhelmed, and crushed like a tiny bug on a big white wall, by the greatness of this awesome Creator. Yet somehow, He didn't. Somehow he didn't see God as a cold, forbidding mountain. When he threw back his head to view God's terrible height and towering splendor, he saw a *fortress.* A hiding place. A warm, secure sanctuary to shelter him from life's threatening storms.

A Quiet Place in a Crazy World

Since you are my rock and my fortress,
for the sake of your name
lead and guide me...
From the ends of the earth I call to you,
I call as my heart grows faint;
lead me to the rock that is higher than I.
For you have been my refuge,
a strong tower against the foe
                              (Psalms 31:3; 61:2-3).

How strong, high, powerful, great, unreachable, lifted up, and secure our God is. And we are the antonym of virtually every one of those adjectives. We are weak, lowly, powerless, impoverished creatures of the dust. Everything that He is, we are not. So why does He tell us those things in the pages of Scripture? Why are we confronted with vista after vista of His might and splendor? So that we will feel crushed and pressed down and trampled in the dust? No...I think He reminds us of our total need and His limitless power to nudge us toward His refuge.

In a crazy world, He is a strong tower. And the door is wide open.

Isn't that what Solomon told us?

"The name of the LORD is a strong tower; the righteous run to it and are safe" (Proverbs 18:10).

LOOK UP!

I can just hear you saying, "Joni, it sounds good, but you have no idea where I'm at in my life. God may be big, but my problems are huge. I try to pray, but sometimes I feel so over-whelmed by it all."

As you know, I loved horseback riding when I was on my feet, especially when I was little. When I finally was big enough to ride my own pony, I just *had* to keep up with my older sisters on their big horses. My problem was that I was only riding a pony half the size of their mounts, so I had to gallop twice as fast to keep up with everybody else.

I didn't mind doing that—I took it as a challenge, until we came to the edge of a river. My sisters always liked to splash ahead, crossing the river at the deepest part. On their big horses, it was fun. But they never seemed to notice that my pony and I were a lot smaller and that we sunk quite a bit deeper into the swirling waters. I was scared, but I wasn't about to let them know.

I'll never forget one river crossing. It was the Marriottsville Crossing where the two branches of the Patapsco River come together. Rain earlier in the week had swollen the river to the brim of its bank. As our horses waded out toward midstream, I stared at the rushing waters that swirled around the shaking legs of my pony. Mesmerized by the circling waters, I felt dizzy. I was frightened and began to lose my balance in the saddle.

My sister—Jay—called back to me. "Look up, Joni—keep looking up!" Sure enough, as soon as I took my eyes off the water and focused on my sister, I regained my balance and finished the river crossing.

That river crossing came to mind recently when I was reading about Peter in Matthew 14. It seems Peter had the same problem when he was walking on the water toward the Lord Jesus. He looked down at the raging waves, got dizzy, and lost his balance. Because he took his eyes off the Lord, he began to sink.

We are so much like Peter! Instead of keeping our eyes on the Word of God, we often let our circumstances transfix us, absorbing us to the point where we lose our spiritual equilibrium. We become dizzy with fear and anxiety. Before we know it, we've lost our balance.

I'm sure there have been times when you've lost your balance in prayer. You try hard to bundle your anxieties and lay them at the feet of Jesus, but you find yourself distracted, absorbed even, by the very concerns you want to pray about.

Am I describing you? Feeling a little panic, are you? Don't know what to do when all your children get sick? Can't seem to adjust to life without wheels while your car is getting a new transmission? Are the books just not balancing this month? Maybe your teenager brought some new "friends" home yesterday, and you're worried about what kind of friends they really are.

It's easy to panic, isn't it? Admittedly, it's hard to look up—especially when you feel like you're sinking. But I made it across the river, and Peter made it back to his boat. Thousands before you have made it through, keeping their eyes on the Lord Jesus. How about you? If you can't find a way out, try looking up. Look up in prayer! And what do you see when you look up? Jesus. Fix your eyes on Jesus.

You may have to keep refocusing your attention, pulling your eyes off the swirling circumstances that overwhelm you in your crazy world. As you steady your gaze upon the Lord, your place of refuge, you will regain your balance. Rest your eyes upon His greatness and majesty, and let your feelings of insecurity begin to ebb away—like a bad dream fades in the golden light of morning.

GOD IS AN EVER-PRESENT REFUGE

To tell you the truth, there are times when I'm relieved, glad even, that I feel small next to God. After all, when you feel small, you want to run to something, someone who is big. It's safe next to a rock, a fortress, a stronghold. You can feel safe in prayer because God is all these strong places to you.

I know something about fortresses. I have happy childhood memories of my sister Kathy and me constructing a tree house on the farm. Our little fortress was some distance from the farmhouse, so it was private and far away from adults. We worked hard lugging wood, confiscating nails, and borrowing hammers to construct a very sturdy tree house.

A shelter? A place to hide? Oh, yes, but it was more than that to me. In my childish thinking it was a *fortress*—a high tower soaring above the wild frontiers! The storms would swirl and howl outside of that little house, the rain would beat on the tin room and the wind would make the house sway in the branches of the tree.

But we were safe. Protected. Dry and cozy.

Don't you ever find yourself wishing it were that easy again? Because the storms don't stop as we grow up, do they? The clouds become darker than we ever imagined and the wind can shake us with a fury that seems more than we can endure. Sometimes, we long for a hiding place.

We're not alone in that desire. Even some of the greatest men of the Bible expressed such a longing. In one of his deepest moments of pain and sorrow over the sin of his people, Jeremiah cried out to God:

Oh, that I had in the desert
A lodging place for travelers,

So that I might leave my people,
And go away from them;
For they are all adulterers,
A crowd of unfaithful people
(Jeremiah 9:2).

There were times when David, too, wished with all his heart
for a shelter from the storms of life.

Oh, that I had the wings of a dove!
I would fly away and be at rest—
I would flee far away
and stay in the desert;
I would hurry to my place of shelter
Far from tempest and storm
(Psalm 55:6-8).

The wonderful thing about the Bible is that it doesn't leave
us in our despair. Scripture tells us that there *is* a hiding place.
A shelter much stronger than a fragile refuge of our own making. Mightier than earth's more powerful citadel.

David wrote:

The Lord is my rock, my fortress and my deliverer; my
God, my rock, in whom I take refuge. My shield and the
horn of my salvation, my stronghold…my God, in
whom I trust! Under his wings you may seek refuge; His
faithfulness is a shield and bulwark… The Lord is with
me; I will not be afraid. What can man do to me? (Psalms
18:2; 91:2,4, NASB; 118:6).

What better hiding place could there be? What better shelter
for anxious hearts and weary minds?

My little tree house taught me a lot about the meaning

behind a "refuge." But like most adults, I put childish things behind me. When I need a refuge now, I come to a Person. In Jesus Christ I have an Everlasting Rock, High Fortress, Mighty Fortress, Tower of Refuge, Shield and Savior.

When the storms of life crowd in, climb up into His love in prayer.

T here's nothing like the furnace blast of dry heat that rises off the surface of the Arizona desert. I was only ten years old and my cow pony and I had become separated from the rest of my family during an afternoon roundup on my Uncle Ted's ranch.

PLACE:
Castle Rock, Arizona

TIME:
Summer 1959

The air sizzled. Even when I strained my eyes, searching the horizon for the others, the distant images only wavered like a mirage. I kicked my pony in the direction of a huge, red boulder. Wiping my brow with my hat, I climbed down to find shelter in the shadow of the rock. Out of the blinding glare, my eyes relaxed. I took a deep breath of the cool air. It was, for me, a place of refuge.

That shadow was also a place of safety and refreshment as I twisted my hat, praying that someone would find me. Only thing was, I had to keep inching over to the left to keep up with the shifting shadow. It was a fickle friend. I didn't mind too much, though. I was just relieved to picture myself, small and insignificant, huddling in the comforting shadow of what felt like Almighty God. It was easier to pray because I felt protected and sheltered.

Within an hour I heard galloping hooves just over the dusty ridge. My family! And just in time. The changing shadow of the rock was about to disappear.

Shadows. Always moving.

Like Jonah crouching under the gourd vine, like a worried little cowgirl huddling beneath a desert boulder, we find shadows fickle friends.

Ah, but the Lord casts an unchanging shadow!

James 1:17 tells us that, "Every good and perfect gift is from above, coming down from the Father of the heavenly lights, who does not change like shifting shadows."

That shadow never shifts, because our Father never changes. He's not evolving, as some theologians would have us believe. He's not transmutable, as other religions profess. No, He is constant and changeless. Always compassionate. Always merciful. Always just. Always holy. Always full of love. Always there.

The shadow of a mighty Rock, within a weary land.

The relief we find in His presence does not change with the passing of the hours, days, or years.

The encouragement we find in His promises will not fail us when the heat of adversity bears down upon us.

The security we find in His character will never vary though our lives turn upside down and the crazy world changes around us.

How wonderful to have His shadow fall across us. Psalm 91 begins by saying, "He who dwells in the shelter of the Most High will abide in the shadow of the Almighty." The psalmist goes on to detail the many ways God protects His own, making them feel secure. In verse 11 we're told, "For He will give His angels charge concerning you, to guard you in all your ways. They will bear you up in their hands, lest you strike your foot against a stone."

Psalm 121 assures us that:
He who watches over you will not slumber;
indeed, he who watches over Israel
will neither slumber nor sleep.
The LORD watches over you—
the LORD is your shade at your right hand;
the sun will not harm you by day,
nor the moon by night.
The LORD will keep you from all harm—
he will watch over your life (vv. 3-7).

If we are willing to put our lives in His hands and our faith in His Word, He will richly reward us by making the passing of each day's shadows a sign of His blessing to come.

You may fail Him, but He will never fail you. Place your chair in the shadow of the cross and you will never have to move it.

YOUR QUIET PLACE...

Right now, recall the last time you found the shelter of shade on a hot day. Remember how rested you felt from the energy-sapping sun? List in your mind those feelings: Unburdened. Relieved. Consoled. Comforted.

Now, that's the way you can feel in the sheltering shade of the Most High God. Rested. Unburdened. Secure. You can breathe in God's shadow.

Take a moment to come before your Place of Refuge in prayer and picture yourself in His protective shadow. Imagine yourself finding a safe place in the cleft of the Rock. Now, fix your eyes on Jesus and bring to Him those problems, those overwhelming circumstances that distract you. Wrap words around those worries of yours and list them one by one as you lay them in His shadow.

Then enjoy that unburdened feeling in His shade. Close your prayer with the psalmist, "He is my refuge and my fortress, my God, in whom I trust" (Psalm 91:2).

CHAPTER THREE

A PLACE OF AWE

*Our prayers must mean something to us
if they are to mean anything to God.*
Maltbie D. Babcock

On the heels of massive upheaval and change in Eastern Europe, barely a few months after the Berlin Wall crumbled, I joined a small group of American disability advocates in a quick blitz through Romania's battle-scarred, but newly-liberated capital city. We were scrambling to seize every opportunity, working feverishly to bring the needs of Romania's desperate, brutally-suppressed disabled population to the attention of that nation's new authorities. We all felt that if we didn't move quickly, the impetus might be lost for yet another generation.

PLACE:
Bucharest, Romania
TIME:
June 1990

Through the American Embassy, I was able to secure a meeting with eight of the new Romanian senators. I would be coming to that meeting as the prominent disability advocate visiting from the United States. Accompanied by Mike Lynch, a former Washington, D.C., embassy attaché, I would come with credentials from America's National Council on Disability and a fresh copy of the landmark Americans with Disabilities Act in hand.

After an exhausting week of puddle jumping to disability events, appointments, and rallies from one end of the country to the other, the day of our meeting with the senators finally arrived.

On a bright, clear morning, we climbed the marble steps of the Romanian senate office building, pausing between the towering Corinthian columns. We knew that all our political know-how, and all our credentials really meant nothing. It's the Lord who has the real power to enact change. It's the Lord who puts kings, presidents, and even senators, on their thrones. It's the Lord whose law has the final word. We huddled between the columns and prayed.

Then, before we stepped through the doors, Mike Lynch gave us a quick lesson on protocol. This is how it would be, this is where we were to sit, this is when we were to speak, this is when we were to listen. He warned us about speaking out of turn, making careless statements, or becoming sloppy in our demeanor. We were in an important meeting place, where we would speak with influential men. Acting foolishly or inappropriately would weaken our appearance and undermine our position. It was imperative that we be at our best.

Sometime after that meeting, I pondered Mike's stern little lesson on protocol. How is it that we never think of those things when we approach Almighty God? He has given us amazing, mind-staggering access into His very presence. Do we abuse that access? Do we rush into His presence unprepared, sloppy in our thoughts, careless in our words, blurting out the first thing that crosses our minds?

Yes, God is our Father. The Lord Jesus is our Lover, Husband, Advocate, and Best Friend.

But He's still the King.

Presidents, pharaohs, sheiks, generals, and kings are subject to Him, and must bow to Him. Should we approach Him with less than our careful respect?

SEEKING GOD WITH CAREFULNESS

Hebrews 13:9 says, "It is good for our hearts to be strengthened by grace." In other words, we're strong when we have God's grace. God's grace is good for our hearts.

But what is grace? Some theologians have said that grace is God's Riches At Christ's Expense. Some commentaries say that grace is God's unmerited favor. Others have described grace as the agent through which God gives us the desire and power to do His will. These are man's best attempts to define what's nearly impossible for us to understand—God's grace.

But how do we get grace? How does God go about dispensing it? Well, it's nice to know that grace is a free gift. But there are a few things to remember as we take hold of His gift. First, God wants us to be humble as we come to Him for grace. After all, Scripture tells us that "God opposes the proud but gives grace to the humble" (James 4:6).

That's important to keep in mind because there are lots of Christians, myself included, who thoughtlessly meander up to God as though He were a doting old grandfather in the sky, giving out grace as He would pass out chocolate chip cookies. You know, the ask-and-it's-ours attitude. What a bunch of spoiled brats we must seem when we ask with a "gimme" mind-set!

APPROACHING AN AWESOME GOD

How, then, should we approach God in prayer?

A popular song reminds us that "our God is an awesome God." He has the power to inspire dread and profound reverence. We should be properly terrified before the Lord our holy God; we should feel wonder and reverent fear.

Job knew the power of his awesome God. As Job desired the presence of his God, he carefully planned how he would order his cause and state his case before the Lord: "Oh that I knew where I might find him!... I would order my cause before him, and fill my mouth with arguments" (Job 23:3-4, KJV). He did not intend to approach God carelessly or with accusations. He understood the significance of prayer and the power of Him who sat on the throne.

There's a widespread notion today that prayer is easy. Too many of us pray carelessly. We have "habitual" prayers that we murmur before bed or at meals, simple little phrases such as "God bless us all and thanks for the food and the good day and forgive us because we've sinned again." We shuffle up to the throne of God, yawning and muttering the first thing that comes to mind. We casually utter our praises, our petitions, our thanksgivings, our supplications—hardly stopping to think before we open our mouths.

There's danger in doing that, I'm afraid, because there is power in what we say before the throne of God's grace. We must approach with a kind of holy carefulness. I learned that lesson the hard way.

B arely three years had passed since I came to Christ at Natural Bridge, Virginia. A lot can change in three years. For one thing, the awesome feeling I had about God—the feeling I experienced on the big flat rock under the stars—had vanished. Little wonder. I had pushed God to a corner of my mind and placed Him in a box labeled, "Break in case of emergency." I went to God as if He were a spiritual vending machine into which I fed dime-like prayers and pulled levers. I didn't know if my requests were spiritual or scriptural. I just casually sauntered up to the throne of God's grace and punched in my requests.

PLACE:
My bedroom in my childhood home, Baltimore

TIME:
April 1967

That attitude got me into trouble. I began to experience discouragement and despondency in my walk with the Lord Jesus. There was no victory over sin for me. I was exasperated, yet my prayers only became more and more self-centered: "Lord, help me lose fifteen pounds now that I'm Your child," or "Lord, help me get through my homework tonight and help it not to be so boring," or "Lord, I sure do like that guy who's captain of the football team. Could You get me a date with him?"

One Friday night, long after midnight, I felt particularly frustrated. I creaked open the kitchen door and sneaked up the back steps to my bedroom. I flicked on the bathroom light, splashed my face with cold water, and stared into the mirror. My eyes were puffy. My lips were swollen. It had been another one of those sordid dates with my boyfriend. I felt dirty and guilty.

I leaned into the mirror and saw an ugly, overweight girl with pimples on her chin. I slipped into my pajamas and threw myself on the bed and cried. I clasped my Bible to my chest and said, "Oh, God, do something in my life, just *do* something. I don't care what happens, but I don't like being miserable!"

I prayed that prayer without knowing how God would answer it. I thought He might give me supernatural power to say "no" to my boyfriend. I thought He would introduce me to a Bible camp counselor that summer who would help me straighten my life out. Maybe I would meet some strong Christian guy who would help me get deeper into God's Word. Or then again, there was a chance I would find a really good fellowship group on my college campus that fall. Perhaps God would make me into a missionary. Maybe I would end up at a Bible college.

To my way of thinking, all these possibilities were reasonable answers to my request to get closer to God. After all, some of my Christian friends had prayed for a closer walk with Jesus, and the Lord had done such things in their lives. So I began looking for the different direction my life would take that last year in high school.

My life *did* take a different direction, but there was no way I could have prepared myself for the surprise—no, the down-right shock—that awaited me.

You see, God took my prayer seriously. About a month later, I dived recklessly into shallow water. When I hit bottom and broke my neck, my life flashed eerily before my eyes, and I knew God was answering that prayer. I was only seventeen years old, but I knew this accident was, in a strange way, the answer to my prayer.

I confess, though, that weeks later as I lay on a Stryker frame in the hospital, facing a life of sitting in a wheelchair without the use of my hands or legs, I fumed, "Great God, this is Your idea of an answer to prayer? Believe me, I will never trust You with another prayer again!"

PETITION WITH CAREFUL RESPECT

Although I wouldn't have called it a legitimate answer to prayer back then, I now see that it was. I can't deny it—God has drawn me closer to Him through my injury. My wheelchair, whether I like it or not, forces me to seek out His Word. It didn't happen through a Bible college or a summer camp. It happened through months of struggling on a hospital Stryker frame. I guess some people have to break their neck to really find God.

But you know what? I can say now I'm *glad* it all happened.

Prayer, as you can see, is serious business. When we approach the throne of God's grace, we have to be careful and approach with holy carefulness…a conscientious piety. If you don't think you need to foster that kind of sharpened attitude toward prayer, let me challenge you with the following example.

Suppose a man receives a traffic ticket he thinks he didn't deserve. He follows instructions on how to appeal the ticket and leaves work in the middle of the day for his scheduled court appearance. Trouble is, he leaves wearing his work clothes—a casual short-sleeved shirt and jeans. He considers the entire affair a waste of time and a capital annoyance.

His attitude is apparent in court. Before the proceedings even begin, he meanders up to the judge's bench, leans on his elbow, cracks his gum, and says to the judge, "Look, you're a nice guy and you gotta understand this whole thing stinks."

The judge looks at the traffic ticket, eyes the well-groomed policeman off to the side, and then stares down at the petitioner. "The citation stands," the judge rules curtly.

The petitioner makes the mistake of rolling his eyes. "Young man, would you like to be held in contempt of court?" the judge demands.

The petitioner gets the message and announces, in a subdued voice, that he would still like to appeal the traffic citation.

In his next court appearance, the man with the traffic ticket wears his best suit. He makes a genuine effort to appear concerned and responsible, he organizes his facts and articulates his side of the story in a polite and thoughtful manner. The traffic ticket is dismissed with no problem. The judge saw his side of the story and justice prevailed.

If you were called into court as a witness or even a defendant, would you stop and think before speaking? Of course. After all, no petitioner enters court thinking that he can state his case on the spur of the moment.

A wise petitioner will enter the chamber with his case well prepared and his ideas well thought out. He wouldn't dare talk off the top of his head. He would never prop his feet up on the railing, lean back in his chair, put his hands behind his head, yawn, or utter the first thing that comes to mind. No, he'd prepare his case or hire a professional lawyer to do it for him.

So why do we often pray so carelessly, even sloppily? Take a look at the Old Testament. The priests who approached God had an attitude of holy carefulness. When they offered sacrifices for the people, they were not to rush into God's presence. The priests would kill the bull, wash their feet, put on garments and special vestments, approach the altar with the bull properly portioned, sprinkle the blood in a certain place, and light the fire a prescribed way with one—and only one—certain kind of match.

Why were the sacrifices so detailed? The underlying truth was simple: Think before you pray.

PRAYERS ARE OFFERINGS, TOO

Our prayers are spiritual sacrifices, too. Often we think of God as a Supreme Being who happily sits by a celestial telephone, only too thrilled when we call and list our demands. I've heard preachers who say, "All you have to do is name it and claim it. You can demand from God what is rightfully yours."

Yes, God may answer demands much as He answered the demands of the children of Israel when they tested Him in the wilderness. He gave them their requests; but remember that He also sent leanness into their souls.

Where do we get this idea that God is overjoyed to comply with our demands? True, God is our best friend, but we dare not take His friendship for granted. Yes, God is happy and willing to hear each of our requests. But the Bible tells us that we are to "worship God acceptably with reverence and awe, for our 'God is a consuming fire' " (Hebrews 12:28-29).

When we acknowledge God as God, we do not "claim." We must not demand. It is better to thoughtfully "let your requests be made known unto God" (Philippians 4:6, KJV). Then we have an attitude of submission, of humility, of deference to the King of kings and Lord of lords.

Yes, there are lots of folks who name it and claim it and demand it and receive it. But frankly, when I look down at this wheelchair, it's a not-so-subtle reminder that God will take very seriously the words we utter before His throne of grace. So it's the wise people who preface prayer with a Thy-will-be-done attitude as they submissively let their requests be made known to God.

MERCY AND GRACE AT THE THRONE

Hebrews 4:16 gives us good advice: "Let us then approach the throne of grace with confidence, so that we may receive mercy and find grace to help us in our time of need." You ought to underline that verse in your Bible if you haven't done so already. It describes the kind of attitude we need to have when we approach God's throne in prayer. Notice the wording: First we receive mercy, then we find grace. That's a great clue as to what our attitude in prayer ought to be.

We may go to God, looking for grace to see us through our problems, but first we must approach our awesome God to receive mercy. Before we obtain answers to our petitions, wants, desires, or requests, we need to humble ourselves so that we may find His favor. That's the attitude we need.

YOUR QUIET PLACE...

Charles Spurgeon said, "He who prays without fervency does not pray at all. We cannot commune with God, who is a consuming fire, if there is no fire in our prayers."

Which of us wouldn't want fire in our prayers? You can have it, you know, when you approach God in careful holiness, first to obtain mercy and then to find grace to help you as you pray.

Right now, imagine yourself in the great throne room of God. Find yourself in the place of awe. Picture the surroundings—the great walls, the tapestries, the throne, the thousands of angels worshiping. Set yourself in the scene as you approach your Almighty God with your praise and petition. Kneel before Him in your heart. Quiet your thoughts. Center your thinking. Focus your words, and then in submission and humility, let your requests be made known to Him.

CHAPTER FOUR

A PLACE OF DUST
AND ASHES

The more we pray, the more we shall want to pray.
The more we pray, the more we can pray.
The more we pray, the more we shall pray.
He who prays little will pray less, but he who prays much will pray more.
And he who prays more, will desire to pray more abundantly.
Charles Haddon Spurgeon

There is a time for simple quietness before the Lord. A time for listening. A time for sitting still. A time to refrain from rushing into God's presence with a tumble of words and requests.

James writes about the need for self-examination and deep humility before our God.

Come near to God and he will come near to you. Wash your hands you sinners, and purify your hearts, you double-minded. Grieve, mourn and wail. Change your laughter to mourning and your joy to gloom. Humble yourselves before the Lord, and he will lift you up (James 4:8-10).

PLACE:
The Girl's Ward,
State Rehab Institute,
Maryland
TIME:
March 1968

For the longest time I tried to twist God's arm so He'd reveal *why* I had my accident. I was banging on the doors of heaven, demanding an answer to prayer, a reason for my horrible plight. I was insistent, almost belligerent, with God.

But all of that haggling and fuming didn't quiet my anxieties—or soothe my fears in the middle of the night when I was alone. I was scared and very distraught.

During those lonely midnight hours I didn't feel so cocky and arrogant in front of God. At those times I pictured Jesus visiting me. I'd imagine Him wearing a rough burlap cloak and a rope belt tied tightly around His waist. My mind's eye saw Him walking softly past the beds of my sleeping roommates, leaving dusty prints from His sandals on the linoleum floor. I'd comfort myself with the image of Him standing at my bedside. I would hear the clunk-clunk of the hospital bed guardrail as He lowered it, and feel His weight as sat on the edge of my bed.

The sharp pain of loneliness eased as I pictured Jesus coming to me in my pain. I saw Him leaning over me, stroking my cheek with the back of His hand, fingering away strands of matted hair from my face.

He would ask me about my day, "How'd it go today, Joni? How was physical therapy? How was your sister? What did she say?" I would picture him visiting me night after night, through long, sleepless hours. Frankly, it was the only thing I could think of that would keep me from crying. I *had* to do this, because I could NOT cry. If I cried, there was no one to blow my nose. There was no one to wipe my tears. It was a horrible, choking, claustrophobic feeling, so I would fight not to cry. Whenever I would feel the tears begin to well up, I had to comfort myself quickly with something. So I would picture the Lord Jesus coming through the door; His shadow from the soft light of the nurse's station.

After our small talk, He would question me, His steady eyes fixed on mine: "Joni, if I loved you enough to die for you, don't you think I knew what I was doing when I answered your prayer for a closer walk with Me?"

His reasoning made sense. If Jesus would die for me, then He could be trusted with everything else He would do with my life. That thought alone humbled me before God. The same God who ladled out seas, carved out rivers, pushed up mountain ranges, and dreamed up time and space cared enough to console me.

It was Peter who wrote, "Humble yourselves, therefore, under God's mighty hand, that he may lift you up in due time" (1 Peter 5:6). Even as I lay there paralyzed, it occurred to me that I had more than enough reason to be grateful. Christ died for me out of love...love I didn't deserve.

What happened after that? God began to answer my prayer for a closer walk with Him. Remember my telling you about that prayer I had so carelessly tossed up just a year earlier? "Oh, God, I want to get close to You"? Only after I humbled myself before the Lord did He begin to lift me up. Slowly and steadily, God began to lift me up out of my anxiety and fear. It didn't happen overnight, but that beginning lift in my lonely room was exactly the push I needed.

DUST AND ASHES

"Now that I have been so bold as to speak to the Lord, though I am nothing but dust and ashes..." (Genesis 18:27).

That was Abraham's attitude when he prayed.

I'm struck with his humility. And the lower Abraham humbled himself, the "higher" he must have felt. I can imagine that when Abraham spoke to God, he felt as though he were carried up on eagle's wings to the heights of heaven. It must have awed him to be allowed, of all things, access to God Almighty. I'm sure even as he spoke to the Lord, he felt as though he were grasping heaven in his arms. He had spoken to the Lord of the universe. That thought alone was enough to lay him lower, reminding him he was mere "dust and ashes."

When I look at Abraham's cry to God—a cry that had nothing to do with a mere arrangement of appropriate words—it's clear that spiritually ordered prayers consist of something more than clustering our requests in a tidy, prescribed fashion.

Spiritual prayers have to do with praying to a real person, someone who is truly present with us even though we cannot see Him. Spiritual praying is conversing with the unseen Creator of the universe as though He were standing visibly and terribly in front of us. That, if anything, will make us feel like Abraham—amazed that we could be bold enough to speak to God.

Certainly there will be times when we pray "on the run," speaking to God sincerely, yet conversationally. We may offer "shotgun prayers"—quick, earnest petitions or intercessions shared hurriedly, yet from the heart. But when it concerns our regular, daily, committed time of prayer, we will want to take time to examine our heart attitude thoroughly, remembering who we are—and who God is.

Picturing ourselves in a place of dust and ashes means *humbling* ourselves; gaining a sense of our meagerness and God's greatness, our sin and His purity, our humanity and His divinity.

Cultivating such an attitude will help us better appreciate God's very real presence with us in prayer. Whether we then "see" Jesus sitting on the side of our bed or grasp heaven as did Abraham, our prayers will seem real. They won't be a mechanical arrangement but will be divinely ordered. We will know the assurance of talking to Someone who is really there.

To let you in on a personal secret, there are times in prayer when I feel too overwhelmed by sin, too earth-stained, too dry or dull to even approach the Father. Don't check me too closely with an open theology book, but when I think of the Father I think of One whose presence demands protocol, formality, and careful choosing of words. You don't just prattle something off the top of your head when you bow before the King of the Universe! It's just not in me, at times like those, to come crawling before His throne, "high and lifted up." I don't want to see the cherubim and the seraphim and His train filling the temple.

Sometimes I don't even have the nerve to speak to the Son. I'm too humiliated, too grieved, too dust-dirty to speak to Jesus. *Fairest Lord Jesus, You have died on the cross for me. You have given me everything. But—I'm sorry, Lord,—You shouldn't even be seeing me like this!*

The Holy Spirit, the One who is called Comforter and Counselor and Guide, seems the most approachable at such times. I ask Him to sit next to me in the dust and ashes as I open up my heart to Him, that Person of the Trinity—that divine Companion—who seems to most understand how I feel. *Here I am, Holy Spirit. In dust and ashes. Licking the dirt. Face down. Covered with soot. Stained. Marred. Like the psalmist before me, "My soul cleaves to the dust." Hear my prayer, dear Counselor.*

In a recent book, Dr. J. I. Packer talks about knowing God "in the fullness of His measure." He affirms the value of communing with and relating to each Person of the Trinity. When it comes to the Holy Spirit, I cling to His nearness, His comfort, His encouragement, His intercession for me with "groans that words cannot express."

At such time you won't hear me pledging my allegiance to God. Instead, I come to Him in empty-handed spiritual poverty with outstretched arms, self-despairing...not boasting so much about my commitment to the Lord, but His commitment to me.

How long has it been since you've felt dust and ashes in prayer? If talking to God doesn't strike you as being one of the most profound, extraordinary privileges imaginable, then perhaps Genesis 18 would be a good place to refresh your prayer life. Only when we feel the dust and ashes can we enter the treasure house of God and embrace heaven.

In praying, we are often occupied with ourselves, with our own needs, and our own efforts in the presentation of them. In waiting upon God, the first thought is of the God upon whom we wait. God longs to reveal Himself, to fill us with Himself. Before you pray, bow quietly before God, to remember and realize who He is, how near He is, how certainly He can and will help. Be still before Him, and allow His Holy Spirit to waken and stir up in your soul the childlike disposition of absolute dependence and confident expectation. Wait on God until you know you have met Him; prayer will then become so different—Andrew Murray

When you pray, do you take at least a moment to think about God before you start speaking to Him? Take time this week to concentrate on God *before* you open your mouth to pray. Realize you are addressing a living and holy Being who is actually listening. And then, confess. Take several moments to think back on your day's misdoings, the small and not-so-small transgressions. Then realize that God, if He were so inclined, could destroy you with His white-hot wrath; yet He has chosen to be kind and merciful. His amazing grace is enough to humble us. He is our loving heavenly Father, full of grace, and we are…dust and ashes.

A PLACE OF HUMILITY

There is no more humbling experience than finding yourself in a place where you are completely dependent on other people for simple tasks such as feeding or bathing yourself. I'm reminded of one young couple I met some years ago.

The young wife tenderly leaned over her husband in the wheel chair. Her husband, severely brain damaged as a result of an automobile accident, lifted his head slightly and smiled. The woman straightened his collar and smoothed his shirt as she talked.

"I used to have a hard time accepting Richard's injury," she said, smiling as she leaned around and looked at him. "And the hardest part was bathing my husband, wasn't it, honey?"

His eyes rolled slightly and he smiled as if to say, "You bet!"

She straightened and fought back tears as she continued. "He would stand in the shower and hold onto the towel rack while I scrubbed his back. All the while my tears mingled with the running water. My big, strong, handsome husband…now he couldn't do for me, I had to do for him. To the point of washing him even."

The man shifted his weight in his wheelchair, unable to speak, only to listen.

"But all of that changed when I realized that Jesus did the same—no, I take that back—He did *much more* when He washed me of the dirt and filth in my own life. Now I count it a privilege to give Richard a bath."

As I listened to this woman's story, reflecting on my own humbling experiences with bathing since paralysis, I was reminded that we are washed every day as believers. The apostle John assures us that "if we confess our sins, he is faithful and just and will forgive us our sins and purify us from all unrighteousness" (1 John 1:9).

In John 13, the Lord got down on His hands and knees and washed the dirty feet of His own disciples.

In Psalm 51 David pled with God to wash him. "Wash away all my iniquity," he prayed, "and cleanse me from my sin...wash me, and I will be whiter than snow...create in me a pure heart" (Psalm 51:2,7,10).

I wonder if David had always had that attitude. I wonder if her ever felt a reluctance about being bathed by somebody else—even if that somebody was God. He may have thought that personal cleansing was something he would have rather done for himself. After all, it could be humiliating to have somebody else take on such private routines. There came a day, however, when King David had no hesitations. He was so soiled, so thoroughly stained by sin and guilt that he fell from his throne and on bended knees cried out to God for cleansing.

The disciples got the picture, too. Even though Peter initially objected to the idea of divine footwashing, he quickly changed his tune as Jesus spelled out the implications. "Then, Lord, not just my feet but my hands and my head as well!" (John 13:9).

The young woman with the brain-damaged husband began to change her attitude toward washing as she realized what her Lord was doing for her every day. God was cleansing away a great deal more dirt and filth from her life than she ever had to face when approaching her husband with a washcloth in hand.

Now, you may not be in a nursing home having to go through bed baths every day. You may not be in bed or ill while others take care of those very intimate needs. But you may be in need of someone—besides yourself—someone who can give you a real cleansing.

If your feet are dirty or your hands are soiled from the everyday contact with this world, come to God in dust and ashes. Let Him wash you, making you whiter than snow. Let Him create in you a clean heart.

YOUR QUIET PLACE...

We come to a place of dust and ashes through the pathway known as Humility. In that place there is no room for high-minded pride. No room for spiritual snobbery.

It's not easy to lay ourselves low before God, but we begin with praise and confession. Have a hard time couching your regret over sin in honest words? Sometimes, it helps to borrow the words of others when humbling ourselves before the Lord.

Pause right now and consider your great and holy God. Then list in your mind five things you've done today that, you believe, offended or grieved Him. Get down in the dust and ashes and share from your heart this confession from the Book of Common Prayer:

Almighty and most merciful Father; We have erred and strayed from thy ways, like lost sheep. We have followed too much the devices and desires of our own hearts. We have offended against thy holy laws. We have left undone those things which we ought to have done; And we have done those things which we ought not to have done; And there is no health in us. But thou, O Lord, have mercy upon us, miserable offenders. Spare thou those, O God, who confess their faults. Restore thou those who are penitent; According to thy promises declared unto mankind in Christ Jesus our Lord. And grant, O most merciful Father, for His sake; That we may hereafter live a godly, righteous, and sober life, To the glory of thy holy Name. Amen.

CHAPTER FIVE

A PLACE OF ASKING

—

If you are sure it is a right thing for which you are asking,
plead now, plead at noon, plead at night, plead on.
With cries and tears spread out your case.
Order your arguments. Back up your pleas with reasons.
Urge the precious blood of Jesus.
Charles Haddon Spurgeon

I t was summer, just prior to the opening of the Los Angeles Olympics, and I had but one burning desire. I was *dying* to see an Olympic torch runner.

The newspaper had said fifty of them would be running predetermined routes scattered across dozens of different locations throughout L.A. and the outlying regions.

PLACE:
Los Angeles,
California

TIME:
July 1984

"Oh Ken," I said, "isn't there *some* place we can go, park on some curbside, and watch a runner go by with a torch? That's all I want! I don't care about platform dives or balance beams or 100-meter dashes. I just want to see the guy carrying the flame!"

Ken is a wonderful, loving husband, but he didn't like that idea one bit. He hates crowds. Hates confusion. Hates delays. Hates traffic.

"Come on, Jon, be realistic! We'd never find a place to park. And it would be so packed with people and cars you wouldn't be able to see him anyway!"

I sighed deeply and—for the moment—let it go.

That Sunday evening we planned to drive into Little Tokyo in downtown L.A. to eat dinner at Ken's favorite hole-in-the-wall Chinese place. I had scanned the Sunday *L.A. Times* to see where the Olympic runner was going to be. I thought maybe, just maybe, he might be downtown at the same time as we were downtown. And maybe *then* I could convince Ken to drive over a couple blocks so we could see him.

The newspaper affirmed that a runner was going to be downtown. In fact, he was going to be running right through Little Tokyo at such and such an hour.

"Now, Ken," I said as sweetly as I could, "if we could leave just an hour early to go to the restaurant, I think we'd be able to make it! We might even be able to get a window seat in the restaurant and—who knows—we may see him actually go by on First Street!"

Ken thought this was absolutely ridiculous. "Joni, *give it up!* You're not going to see the guy with the torch. Besides, you can watch it all on TV."

I didn't say any more, but I did take the route map with me, hoping against hope that we would catch a glimpse of the Man With The Flame.

We got there too late. Ken didn't want to fight the crowds. He didn't want to hassle the parking. So I choked down my Kung Pao beef in disgust and disappointment, because I wasn't going to see the runner.

Suddenly I looked my husband in the eye.

"Ken," I told him, "I'm going to *pray*, and ask the Lord if I can please see the runner. That's all I want! Just to see the guy with the torch."

Ken just shook his head, paid the bill, and we went out the door.

It wasn't long before we were cruising through the Sepulveda Pass on the San Diego Freeway, headed home to Agoura Hills. I glanced at my route map. According to the schedule, a runner would have paralleled this very stretch of freeway, over six hours before.

Suddenly we saw brakelights. Lots and lots of them. "Oh, no," Ken groaned. "What's with all this traffic on a Sunday night? The runner ran through this stretch hours and hours ago!"

And I thought, *Oh, no he didn't! He's late! And we're going to see him!*

There is a frontage road that for about one hundred feet parallels the San Diego Freeway. The chances of traversing the freeway at twenty miles per through slow traffic at the precise moment when the runner jogged down that tiny stretch of frontage road were a million to one. But the Lord did it for me!

We actually *paced* the runner for about one hundred feet. He was just thirty feet away from the passenger window of the car, the flame of the uplifted golden torch illuminating a noble, determined face. Helicopters with spotlights hovered overhead. Police cars with flashing lights went in front of him and behind him.

But we drove right alongside.

I looked into his face. I saw his sweat. I saw his muscles. I saw him lift his torch. I heard his breathing. I heard the crunch of gravel under his feet. I heard the applause.

"Ken...KEN!" I screamed. "Look at this! LOOK AT THIS!"

A Place of Asking

Ken simply couldn't believe his eyes. How had we "happened" to be in the right-hand lane of six lanes of traffic at the precise instant when the flame-bearer turned the corner of the frontage road he had supposedly traversed six hours previous? It was impossible and yet...my Father heard the wistful prayer of His daughter; the simple request of one who had come to a place of asking.

From that day on, Ken *never* discounts my prayers. He even checks in with me before he goes fishing!

It's morning. It's before I've seen anybody. And out on this freeway, it's a conversation with God. I don't dare pull into the parking lot, turn off the ignition, and wheel into the office without "asking" something of God concerning the day.

It's sincere.

It's specific.

PLACE:
My morning commute to Agoura Hills

TIME:
9:30 A.M.

It's about the people I will meet that day, the phone calls, the letters answered, the co-workers I see passing through the front door. It's about asking the Holy Spirit to nudge me through every hour of the day, reminding me that I require fresh grace for each moment. It's about a conscious acknowledgment that I *must* move in the Spirit, not in the flesh, if anything is to be accomplished for the kingdom.

"Asking," wrote E. Stanley Jones, "is the symbol of our desire. Some things God will not give until we want them enough to ask." Asking is also a kind of expressed dependence. A daily dependence. Give us *this day* our daily bread. An unknown preacher said, "We are to ask with a beggar's humility,

A Quiet Place in a Crazy World

to seek with a servant's carefulness, and to knock with the confidence of a friend."

BE SPECIFIC IN ASKING

When we are specific in prayer, God "is able to do immeasurably more than all we ask or imagine, according to his power that is at work within us" (Ephesians 3:20). Isn't that marvelous? God wants to do so much more than we could ever ask. When we buckle down and get specific, our sovereign God will do far more than we could imagine.

A number of years ago I was invited by the Billy Graham Evangelistic Association to lead two workshops during an international congress on Third World evangelism in Amsterdam. There were evangelists from over 160 countries, including Malawi, Bangladesh, India, the Solomon Islands, Western Samoa, and the Philippines. It was incredible!

Our workshops on sharing Christ with those who are disabled were wonderfully well attended. Between sessions, I was almost hit broadside by an excited evangelist with dark olive skin and a bushy beard. In a thick Middle Eastern accent, he said, "Oh, I must tell you that I am from Iran, and I must tell you that my friends and I translated your books into the Persian language and have been sharing them faithfully with handicapped people in Tehran."

It was all I could do not to cry right in front of the man. When I wrote *Joni* and *A Step Further*, I thought maybe a few disabled people like me, in wheelchairs, could benefit from the message. I figured my relatives might buy a copy. But when that evangelist from Iran told me about a Persian version of my book, it really made me think. I wish I had been a lot more specific in my prayers about the ministry of those books when they were first published. Yet God was doing far more than I could ever ask or even imagine, turning my small, specific request into a grand answer!

BE SURE WHEN YOU ASK

Being specific in prayer is one thing, being *sure* is another.

Many times we waffle and waver in prayer, not feeling certain that what we are asking for is in line with God's will. Are we asking with God's highest glory in mind, or is that the faint voice of the Holy Spirit we're trying to ignore? Are we magnifying the Lord with our requests or…manipulating Him? How can we be certain, even confident in asking?

Consider the story of Jacob—the man who wrestled with God. You'll find it in Genesis 32:2-28. Jacob grappled with his divine Visitor through the night until daybreak. As the sun began to creep up over the horizon, God touched Jacob's hip—actually wrenching it out of its socket.

The Wrestler said, "Let me go, for it is daybreak."

But Jacob replied, "I will not let You go unless You bless me."

Because Jacob persevered, God changed Jacob's name to Israel, because he had "struggled with God and with men and…overcome."

Have you struggled with something until you were sure it was God's will? Have you persevered in prayer because you know it is right? Charles Spurgeon said:

It is delightful to hear a man wrestle with God and say, "I will not let Thee go except Thou bless me," but that must be said softly, and not in a hectoring spirit, as though we could command and exact blessings from the Lord of all. Remember, it is still a man wrestling, even though permitted to wrestle with the eternal I AM. Jacob halted on his thigh after that night's holy conflict, to let him see that God is terrible, and that his prevailing power did not lie in himself. We are taught to say, "Our Father," but still it is, "Our Father who art in heaven." Familiarity there may be, but holy familiarity; boldness, but the boldness which springs from grace and is the work of the Spirit; not the boldness of the rebel who carries a brazen front in the presence of his offended king, but the boldness of the child who fears because he loves, and loves because he fears. —Charles Haddon Spurgeon, Lectures to My Students.

I like Martin Luther's prayer: "Lord, I will have my will of Thee at this time, because I know it is Thy will." Have you ever been able to pray that way? When we are sure what we are asking is for God's glory, not for selfish gain or impure motives, then we can say with Jacob, "I will not let Thee go except Thou bless me." It's a risky prayer, isn't it? Some people have broken their necks finding God. Other people like Jacob have had their hips thrown out of socket. But ah, the blessings that come!

YOUR QUIET PLACE...

Are there specific questions you want to ask God? Specific areas you need God's help in? Take time now to list them. Then talk to God about them one by one. "Wrestle" with Him over them if you have to. Ask Him to show you His will in each point. Be open to the changes God may bring in your life.

A Place of Asking

CHAPTER SIX

A PLACE OF DISCIPLINE

I believe that when we cannot pray,
it is time that we prayed more than ever.
And if you answer, "But how can that be?" I would say,
pray to pray. Pray for prayer. Pray for the spirit of supplication.
Do not be content to say, "I would pray if I could."
No, but if you cannot pray, pray till you can.

Charles Haddon Spurgeon

C hristians who can pray everywhere all the time, do so because they can pray somewhere some of the time. I'm convinced it was even that way for Jesus.

The Lord was able to pray in the morning or late at night, here, there, and everywhere. But I would like to think He also disciplined Himself to pray in one special place most of the time. Perhaps that place was the Garden of Gethsemane. There, outside the walls of the Holy City, He probably met often with the Father, whether in the cool hours of dawn or the soft shadows of moonlight.

PLACE:
My bedroom on any
night this year

TIME:
7:30 to 9:30 P.M.

In fact, on one of those evenings He invited His disciples to pray with Him. It meant the discipline of an entire hour of praise and intercession and petition. But His weary friends were overcome by sleep. Jesus nudged them awake and lamented,

"Could you not watch with Me one hour?"

I like to imagine I would have tiptoed over the sleeping forms of the disciples and boldly joined Jesus kneeling there at the rock, clasping my hands earnestly in prayer, keen-spirited, sharp-minded, ready to do spiritual intercession with Him.

That's what I would *like* to do. But big disciplines have to start small.

I have determined that my bed is to be my place of prayer. Ken helps me out of my chair and lays me down around 7:30 every evening, and that means I have plenty of time. How blessed I am because of my disability! Other wives are doing the second load of laundry, folding towels, or putting the third kid to bed at 7:30. And *I* am paralyzed in bed. What a privilege!

My bedroom is my place of prayer. A quiet place, softly lit. No music. No TV. It's a *meeting* place. Because of that, I'm always conditioned now to move into a prayer mode as soon as my head touches the pillow. If there's a breeze outside, I hear the wind chimes tinkle by the sliding glass door. Ken occasionally leaves his work at the desk to come in and check on me. Scruffy may curl up at the edge of the bed and softly snore. The clock ticks and I watch time breeze by when I pray.

There is a time of praise, of waiting, of confession, scripture praying, watching, interceding, petitioning, thanksgiving, singing and meditating, listening, and then ending with more praise. It's a way of dividing an hour into five-minute segments. Five minutes of praise, five minutes of scripture praying, five minutes of waiting, *never* five minutes of intercession—it always ends up being about a half an hour of intercession and everything else gets squeezed down.

On some evenings, I "feel" nothing during those hours...but

the real satisfaction is in doing the work of interceding. You don't have to have feelings for that, just commitment.

My bed used to be a "bed of affliction," because as a quadriplegic, gravity is my enemy. I am more paralyzed lying down than at any other time. It used to be a terrifying thing to lie down at night. It used to make me feel more confined and disabled and claustrophobic and *limited.*

No longer. Now it's my favorite place to be. I'm kneeling with Jesus in the Garden. We're at that rock together. I'm interceding with Him. I'm watching with Him for an hour, two hours, three hours. And sometimes I can't wait to meet Him there.

People often say to me, "How do you keep your composure? Your life is so busy and fast-paced." It's true. My schedule is hectic. I have many responsibilities. I travel more than most. I do spend a lot of time rushing here, there, and everywhere, and, like every other believer, I must face Scripture's admonishment to "be still and know that I am God." But in my life, there is always a big part of me that *is* still, that never, ever moves. There is an *enforced* stillness in my life—and I carry it with me everywhere! And that, I've come to learn through these twenty-six years of paralysis, is a *blessing.*

All beds "feel" the same to me, because I can't feel them. So it doesn't matter if I'm in a bed in Bucharest or Quito or Manila or Moscow. Wherever I am, physical necessity says I must lie down by 7:30. God knows that here is a person He can count on every night at the same time! Here is a lady who, in spite of herself, will always keep her appointment!

I tell the Lord in prayer, "Now, Lord, here I am on this bed again. It is flat. It is rectangular. It has four legs. It is an altar, and on it is Your sacrifice of praise, from which my fragrant incense of intercessions arise."

But the secret, I'm afraid, is out. *It really isn't a sacrifice anymore*. It's a deep and overflowing joy.

PRAYER IS AN ART

Although prayer is an art which only the Holy Spirit can teach us, I think it's important to pray until you know how to pray. Pray to be helped in prayer. Prayer is not something we can learn through reading a book.

It is something we develop when we come to a place of discipline.

It is hard work.

But like any discipline that at first seems hard, it then becomes an art. Yes, prayer can move from a teeth-gritting disicipline to a kind of art form that flows in effortless beauty.

"Get real, Joni," I can hear some saying. "You'll never convince me that prayer is anything but hard work."

Well, please bear with me as I give a little art lesson here.

Have you ever wondered how it is that people spend thousands, even millions of dollars on paintings by the masters? Have you ever scratched your head and thought that people who stand for hours in front of a Monet are a little bit strange? Have you ever looked at a modern sculpture and thought, *I'm missing something here?* Have you ever wondered why an Ansel Adams photograph can speak volumes? What do people see in art, anyway?

Perhaps you're more mystified by music. Does it seem strange to you that some people spend hundreds of dollars to buy season tickets to a symphony? That they can sit and listen for hours to a Mendelssohn concerto? Aren't they going a little bit overboard?

I remember when I had a "ho-hum" attitude toward art. I used to look at certain sculptures and snicker. I would visit museums and see people standing for long periods of time in front of paintings, and I knew I was somehow missing the point.

But my attitude began to change when I met my art teacher. Before I even picked up my brush in our daily art lessons, we would spend an hour looking through art books. My art teacher would pause at a print by Monet, and we'd discuss the color and composition. He would flip the page, and we'd look at prints by Cezanne or Gauguin. We'd discuss color tests, the experiments, the values of light and dark, the hues of the various shades of pink and blue.

At first I felt...well, bored. But the more I looked and listened, the more I began to appreciate. Spending time with those masters, page after page, began to elevate my thinking. The more I looked at works of art, the more frequently I visited museums. The more I visited museums, the more that was revealed. The more that was revealed, the more I understood. The more I understood, the more I felt joy. Now when I see people studying a Rembrandt, I understand what they are appreciating. The key is this: If you don't appreciate good art, then spend time looking at good art. If you don't appreciate good music, spend long hours listening to good music.

I know people who have a similar struggle when they look at the prayer habits of others. They listen to someone who's excited about spending a morning talking to the Lord, and they scratch their heads and yawn and think, *Well that's fine for them, but I just don't get it. I just don't see why they enjoy praying—maybe I'm missing something.*

Ever feel that way? Perhaps you could never imagine yourself as a "prayer warrior." You think certain people must be better equipped, maybe they're better trained, or their personalities lend themselves to prayer better than yours does. But frankly, the only way you and I can develop a real appreciation for prayer is to pray. Prayer itself is an art which only the Holy Spirit can teach.

Pray for prayer.

Pray to be helped in prayer.

Pray until you appreciate prayer.

Prayer is very much like other disciplines. Like art and music it is a discipline that can only be appreciated when you actually spend time in it. Spending time with the Master will elevate your thinking. The more you pray, the more will be revealed. You will understand. You will smile and nod your head as you identify with others who fight long battles and find great joy on their knees.

We can't afford to neglect the discipline of prayer, no more than a soldier can afford to take a vacation from boot camp.

The more you pray, the more you will be like Abraham, who felt as though he was dust and ashes. You will be like Jacob, who said, "I will not let you go until you bless me." You will be prepared to face what lies ahead in life. The more you pray, the more you will understand, the more joy you will have, and the more you will know the greatness of our God.

YOUR QUIET PLACE...

If you are earnest about seeking God, you should be earnest about prayer. Take a moment now to pray. Put this book down, close your eyes, still your heart, and quiet your thoughts. Remember the place of dust and ashes.

Kneel before God in your imagination on the floor of the

throne room. Approach with awe and reverence and a holy kind of carefulness. God is very real, and we should be humbled that He delights in hearing our requests, that He welcomes our words, and that He is happy to hear what we say. But we can't take that kind of freedom for granted. We should simply lift holy hands before Him, hands made clean through the blood of Jesus Christ, and say, "Father, we praise You, we adore You, we extol You, we magnify and glorify You."

For several minutes, speak to God about speaking with God. Keep your conversation with Him specifically about prayer. Ask Him to help you pray until you can pray, until you appreciate the discipline, the art, of prayer. Ask Him to help you understand because He promises to reveal, and in so doing you will receive joy. Pray in Jesus' name, and thank Him for welcoming you into His family. Praise God for Jesus and for listening to your prayer because of Jesus. Thank Him for meeting you in your quiet place, and for bringing you to a place of discipline that will help you draw closer to Him.

CHAPTER SEVEN

A PLACE OF LISTENING

In quietness and in confidence shall be your strength...
Study the quiet
(Isaiah 30:15; 1 Thessalonians 4:11, KJV).

Speak LORD,
for your servant is listening
(1 Samuel 3:9).

My computer has company this morning. But then, it has company every morning. A Bible rests on top of the hard drive. A hymnal leans companionably against the monitor. A well-thumbed *Book of Common Prayer* lies within easy reach on a shelf above. On a lower shelf, flanking the keyboard, a book of Christian poetry props up against a volume on the names of Jesus.

PLACE:
In my office,
in front of
my computer

These are tools that help me listen to God.

TIME:
Most any morning

As in anyone's day, I'm constantly shifting gears from one task to the next. But I dare not rush between jobs without pausing to thank God for what was just completed...and to ask Him for guidance on what is to be done next.

That means pausing to listen.

That means raising my spiritual antennae to discern His clear directional signal.

How do we do that here at the office? Maybe Francie and I will flip open the hymnal and harmonize on "My Faith Looks Up to the Thee." Or we'll grab a co-worker on her way to the Xerox machine as she passes by the office door, and have her join us on a verse of "Great Is Thy Faithfulness." We'll take a moment to consider one of the names of Jesus. *Counselor. Word of God. Bread of Life. Ancient of Days.* Then maybe we'll take a long sip of coffee, hold hands, and pray...which always includes keeping "ears tuned" to what the Lord thinks ought to be accomplished in the next task, whether it's an article or a letter or a radio program or part of a manuscript.

You might call it priming the pump. I call it listening to God.

I listen for His voice. I wait. I take the time. And He has never failed to meet me at that place of listening. He gives me instructions. Impressions. Convictions. Directions. Gentle rebukes. Affirmations. He whispers, "This is the way, walk ye in it. No, don't turn to the left. Don't turn to the right. Don't turn back. Come straight ahead, and I will be with you."

It's the same in my painting studio. I wheel into the room and the illustration board stares back at me...big, blank, white, scary. It's intimidating. It's frightening. I sometimes feel suddenly weak, or dull, as if I could never come up with another idea as long as I live.

"Oh, God," I whisper, "help me! What do I do? What do You want me to do?"

And in the quietness of my little studio, I do very much the same as in front of my blank computer screen. I read some scripture. Sing a hymn. Murmur a prayer. Listen to some classical music. Leaf through some big art books, letting my eyes linger on the works of the masters. Surround myself with color. And then…listen. I just listen for His voice. I wait to see where He wants me to begin, what He wants me to do.

I wheel back away from the easel, so I won't be tempted to charge in and start throwing paint around prematurely. I let the room become very, very silent. And wait. And wait. Until I hear something. And then I say, "Yes. *Yes*. Of course. That's the way I want to begin. This is the way it should be."

Waiting for God to speak can be stretching at times. In different places around the world, I have been backstage waiting for my introduction, and really not certain of what I was supposed to say. Days before my speaking engagement I ask Him again and again, "What do You want me to communicate here? What do these people need to hear from You?" As the engagement draws near and He doesn't tell me, it gets tense. And there have been times—an hour before I have to speak—in my hotel room, when I cry out to Him, "But Lord, You haven't *told* me yet what You want me to say!"

Yes, the answer comes. The words are there when I need them. But not always when I *want* them!

To listen in prayer is to mentally absorb divine instructions concerning the matters of the day. To listen is to not take the day in one fell swoop, but in hourly or even moment-by-moment increments. The day's schedule which looked organized in the morning can, like a deck of cards, be shuffled by noon. Circumstances can shift. Plans can change. That's why keeping your heart's ear cocked hour by hour is so important.

Listening implies confidence that God truly desires to speak with us. Only as we learn to hear the voice of the Father can we learn to shut our ears to the voices of the world.

It's always easy to hear our own voices, because we are basically selfish people. But it's a matter of tuning—fine-tuning the ear of the heart—to discern God's desires and intentions. It means, as Scripture says, *inclining your ear* to what He has to say, just as He inclines His ear to our prayers. When I think of God hearing my prayer, I sometimes imagine a little girl pulling on her dad's trouser leg. And that big man gets down on his knees and looks in to his little daughter's eyes, and says, "I'm listening. What is it, honey?" If that's the way God listens to my voice, I want to hear every word that He has to say, too.

Our usual tendency is to march into prayer with our own agenda, assuming that whatever is on God's heart will for certain match what's on ours. To be honest, our tendency is to not even be concerned about His heart's desire for our prayer time—thus, our lack of interest in listening.

We cover over His voice with a lot of noise and frenzy and motion. We hear the Holy Spirit speaking a quiet word to our heart, but then finish His sentence assuming we've caught His drift. Or we receive His message but are too busy or too distracted to make sense of it. We tell ourselves we'll go back and double-check it later, but by the time we get around to it, the moment is gone. The voice is silent. The opportunity is passed.

For many of us, prayer has become a one-sided, one-dimensional recitation of our needs and wants and thoughts. And yes, it's true, He loves to hear us speak. But He also loves to speak in return.

That's the way it is with best friends.

YOUR QUIET PLACE...

You may not be an artist or a writer. You may not face a blank canvas or blank computer screen every morning. But each new day before us is a "blank," isn't it? And each one of us, no matter who we are, face a hundred different tasks a day. Between each of those tasks, even though the time is short, there is time to listen to God. There is time to bend our antennas to His signal. Do that today. Try it. Before you write that letter...before you make that call...before you get out of the car...before you pick up whatever you need to pick up to do whatever you need to do...take a moment to come to a place of listening. Consider your Lord, who is interested in every detail of your day. Pause to acknowledge Him, and cock your ear to listen for His voice.

You've dialed His number again and again. Are you ready to take His return call?

CHAPTER EIGHT

A PLACE TO PLEAD
YOUR CASE

Do not reckon you have prayed unless you have pleaded,
for pleading is the very marrow of prayer.
Charles Haddon Spurgeon

W hen my husband and I argue, I have to admit that Ken
is a fair fighter. He usually gets angry without getting
destructive. He fights—but he fights fairly.

Except, the other night he pulled a fast one. We
were arguing in the living room, and our discussion was going rather smoothly—for an argument, that is. But his temper got a little hot when
I let some stupid remark slip. That did it. Ken
stomped out of the living room and slammed the
door. Do you know what that meant? I was
unable to follow him. I physically could not open
the living room door to follow him into the kitchen. I was stuck.

To me, that was fighting unfairly. Well, I put a lid on my
own temper, lowered my voice, and politely reminded Ken
that shutting doors was a low blow. With that, the living room

PLACE:
The Tada home
in Calabasas,
California
TIME:
7:00 P.M.

door slowly cracked open, and I was able to wheel into the kitchen where, I'm glad to tell you, our silly argument was resolved.

Fighting fair? It's essential if you and your spouse—or your friend or roommate—are going to be able not only to air your differences but honestly deal with them. And it's a good principle to remember when approaching God with your reasons and convictions. He gives you a place to plead your case. But there are rules for presenting a good argument.

First, remember to *argue*, not quarrel. When Ken and I argue, we first bite our tongues, then we sit down and begin to reason. I have to promise to listen with an open heart and an open mind for an entire fifteen minutes. I can't interrupt. I can't interject. I can't defend myself. I promise to listen, knowing that after fifteen minutes, Ken will be quiet and I will get to share my point of view. That's when I have an opportunity to share my case, give good reasons, and point to the evidence.

Back and forth we go until we resolve the conflict.

My wheelchair has helped us learn how to handle our anger properly. I can't stomp out of the house, slam the door, get in the car, and roar down the street to a friend's house. It's not as though I can lock the bedroom door and go to bed early, pull the covers over my head, and turn my back on my husband in disgust. About the worst thing I can do to my husband is run over his toes!

So I hope you can understand how we relate to what Paul wrote in 2 Corinthians 12:9-10: "Therefore I will boast all the more gladly about my weaknesses, so that Christ's power may rest on me. That is why, for Christ's sake, I delight in weaknesses, in insults, in hardships, in persecutions, in difficulties. For when I am weak, then I am strong."

My wheelchair is an asset to us rather than a liability. If anything, it has taught us how to argue.

WHAT DOES IT MEAN TO "REASON"?

I love words. I think it's fascinating to find out the meaning and origin of a word.

Consider the word *argument*. Most of us immediately think of a quarrel, don't we? We imagine a rousing ruckus where two angry people spew forth a torrent of hot, biting words, eventually ending up throwing things around the room.

But *argument*, from a root word meaning "to make clear or to reason," is partially defined by Webster's dictionary as "a proof or rebuttal, a coherent series of reasons offered." In other words, to argue is to offer reasons, to give evidence. When people argue, they offer proofs supporting their convictions.

Argument, then, is rather a good word!

When you think about it, there are many stories in the Bible of great men of faith arguing with the Lord. Job argued before God, but he did not quarrel. Anger had nothing to do with his argument. He simply desired to present himself and his convictions before the Lord.

DON'T ARGUE IN ANGER

Marriage has taught me a lot about the meaning of the word *argument*. I've been married almost twelve years, and I don't pretend to be an expert on marriage, but with my disability my husband and I have learned a lot about how to argue.

It's inevitable that a marriage partner is going to get angry.

A Place to Plead Your Case

At some point, someone in the marriage is going to get their feelings bruised over unmet expectations or inevitable misunderstandings. Anger will raise its stubborn head. Now anger itself is not a sin, but the Bible makes it clear that we had better handle anger properly so that we don't sin.

The worst way to handle anger is to quarrel. Quarreling, unlike arguing, is an explosive shouting match, a hot-tempered contest to see which one of you can throw the biggest barbs. I know that when I have quarreled I have felt as though I were reading a bad script: "You never do this!" "You always do that!" "It really makes me mad when you..." Sound familiar?

Quarreling is the wrong way to handle anger. Instead, God would have us argue.

GIVING GOD YOUR REASONS

To argue, then, is *to offer reasons* or *to give evidence*. When someone argues, he puts forth proofs of his convictions. Do you remember what Job said? "If only I knew where to find him; if only I could go to his dwelling! I would state my case before him and fill my mouth with arguments" (Job 23:3-4).

If you believe strongly enough about a concern that you would bring it before God in prayer, be prepared to offer an argument, a reason why you feel the Lord would be glorified through your request. Fill your mouth with a good case statement, not flattery or fancy phrases or pat petitions you may have said scores of times before. To argue is to take the time and thought to offer reasons to God.

I admire "argumentative" prayer. I think God is pleased to listen to someone who takes his prayer seriously enough to contend for what he believes. Remember, God said to Isaiah,

"Come now, let us reason together" (Isaiah 1:18).

God asks us to plead with Him, to seriously weigh our words when we come into His presence, to bring forth our pros and cons, to put deep thought into our prayer. As Spurgeon said, "When a man searches arguments for a thing, it is because he attaches importance to that which he is seeking." And God loves a man who will converse with Him like that.

But why should we argue at all? Well, it's obviously not because God needs to be informed. He knows the reasons for our circumstances, and He knows more about our situation than we do. There is nothing we could tell God that He doesn't already know. We don't argue because God is lacking information. We don't argue because He is slow to give and has to be pushed and prodded to do His will. No. We argue not for His benefit but for ours.

We are to involve ourselves in our prayers, to test our thoughts in order to see if a thing is truly of the Lord and His will. To paraphrase it, God inasmuch said to Isaiah, "Come now put on your thinking cap and let's reason this thing out *together*. Engage yourself in prayer, Isaiah, and let Me know that you're attaching importance to everything you're saying." The Lord delights in having His children come to Him that way. God wants us to involve ourselves in prayer. He wants us not simply to talk to Him but to converse with Him.

The Lord tells you to come and reason with Him. God issued the invitation to Isaiah, and He extends the same invitation to you today.

S ome years ago I was sent by my publisher on a national tour to help promote a book I had just completed. That meant plenty of bookstore parties and plenty of people waiting in long lines for my autograph.

I felt badly that it was taking me so long to auto-graph all those books—you see, I have to write with a pen between my teeth and I can't talk to people and write at the same time.

PLACE:
A bookstore in Grand Rapids, Michigan

TIME:
October 1987

Anyway, in the long line there stood a girl about ten years old. She was clutching a tattered copy of my first book, *Joni*. In a shy voice she said, "My name is Kitty. I read this when I was a little girl. It means a lot to me because I have a heart disease, and I can't go out and play with my friends. And Joni, I don't know…I've got a lot of questions for God."

At that point it was all I could do not to cry. I noticed her mother patting her shoulder. I didn't have time to talk privately with Kitty's mother then, but in my heart I prayed, *Dear God, please let that mom allow her daughter to have questions.*

As Kitty looked up at me with those liquid blue eyes, my thoughts flashed back to those early days when, like her, I had a lot of questions for God. Back then, I was comforted to real-ize that the God of the Bible was not human-sized, but God-sized. He could handle my toughest questions. God was not intimidated by my interrogation or threatened by my doubts. In fact, at times I almost sensed God saying, "Come now, Joni, let's reason together. Put your thinking cap on. Let's work this problem out."

I leaned down to Kitty and I said, "Don't be afraid of your questions. Our God is big enough to handle your biggest

A Quiet Place in a Crazy World

doubts. In fact, there was even a man in the Bible who said, 'Lord, I believe. Help my unbelief.' And, Kitty, that's what you're doing when you talk to God. You believe in Him simply because you're talking to Him. But be honest enough to share your questions and concerns. He won't be intimidated. He'll love talking with you."

A wide-eyed look of wondrous revelation spread across Kitty's face. When she smiled, it was as though a bright light dawned above her head as she realized God was not afraid of her questions. For that matter, she didn't have to be afraid of presenting her heartfelt concerns to the Lord. He knew them anyway. Why shouldn't Kitty be honest with Him and share what was on her heart? She needed to be consoled not to smother her querying, but to think through her faith until she could better understand the character of God and His response to her questions.

I can identify with Kitty.

When I was first injured, my mind swirled with questions. When I learned that my paralysis was going to be permanent, it raised even more questions. Desperate to find answers, I turned to the book of Job.

GOD EXPECTS QUESTIONS

Job, I reasoned, had suffered terribly and questioned God again and again. Perhaps I could find comfort and insight from following his search for answers.

Frankly, it's ironic that many Christians turn to Job for help and comfort. In reality, the book raises more questions than it answers. You'll look in vain through its pages for neat, compact theories on why people suffer. God not only refuses to answer

Job's agonizing questions, He also declines to comment on all the tidy theological theories offered by Job's erstwhile friends.

And make no mistake, Job's questions to God weren't of the polite Sunday school variety. They were pointed, sharp, and seemed at times on the border of blasphemy.

Why didn't You let me die at birth? (3:11).

Why didn't You dry up my mother's breasts so that I would starve? (3:12).

Why do You keep wretched people like me alive? (3:20-22).

How do You expect me to have hope and patience? (6:11).

What do You think I'm made of, anyway? Stone? Metal? (6:12).

If life is so short, does it have to be miserable, too? (7:1-10).

Why don't You back off and quit hurting me for awhile? (7:17,19).

What did I ever do to You that I become the target for Your arrows? (7:20).

Why don't You forgive me before I die and it's too late? (7:21).

How can mortal man be righteous before a holy God? (9:2).

Why do You favor the wicked? (9:24).

Since You've already decided I'm guilty, why should I even try? (9:29).

You're the One who created me, so why are You destroying me? (10:8).

Why do You hide Your face and consider me Your enemy? (13:24).

Why don't You let me meet You somewhere face to face so I can state my case? (23:3-6).

Why don't You set a time to judge wicked men? (24:1).

Tough, searching questions. Job's friends were horrified. They half expected lightning to fall and fry the suffering man on the spot.

But the lightning never fell.

And that, to me, is the comfort of the book of Job. What meant the most to me in my suffering was that God never condemns Job for his doubt and despair. God was even ready to take on the hard questions. Ah, but the answers? They weren't quite the ones Job was expecting.

Likewise, when it comes right down to it, I'm not sure if it would have sufficed to find "the answers" anyway. What if God had suddenly consented to answer all my queries? Could I have even begun to handle it? It would have been like pouring million-gallon truths into a one-ounce container. Dumping a water tower into a child's play tea cup. My poor pea brain wouldn't have been able to process it.

For some odd reason, however, it comforted me to realize that God did not condemn me for plying Him with questions. I didn't have to worry about insulting God by my outbursts in time of stress and fear and pain. My despair wasn't going to shock Him. God, according to the book of Job, cannot be threatened by questions from Job...or Joni...or Kitty...or you. God can handle any question you have.

The next time you find yourself in a perplexing situation that demands prayer, discuss with God how you think He might be glorified in the situation. Present to Him the reasons you think He should move or act out His will. Tell Him how you believe His kingdom will be advanced, His people encouraged, His Word honored. Let Him know that you have searched to find His heart. Let Him know that you want to plead with Him and, in so doing, let Him see that you are attaching great importance to the request you are presenting before His throne. And don't forget to argue fairly—keep your mind open for change and be sure to listen to Him. After all, God will have a thing or two to say to you in this argument!

YOUR QUIET PLACE...

Think of a request or an intercession you have recently brought before the Lord in prayer. It could be something as simple as:

"Lord, will You please bring a helper into the life of my neighbor with a disability. She has so many needs and can't go it alone."

Now, list five good reasons for your request. They could include:

1. Lord, You were compassionate toward disabled people when You walked on earth and You met their needs. Please meet the needs of my friend that way.

2. Lord, You promised to feed the ravens and clothe the flowers of the field. My disabled neighbor has basic needs like that, and You care much more for her than You do for the birds and flowers.

3. Lord, my neighbor is in need of seeing and feeling Your personal care. A helper could be Your "hands" to her.

4. Lord, You cared about "the least of the brethren," and my disabled neighbor certainly qualifies under that category! Please meet her need as an evidence of Your concern for the least of the brethren.

5. Lord, the rest of my neighbors will be inspired and encouraged to help, and they may even "know we are Christians by our love for one another."

Got the picture? Get out a pencil, a pad of paper, and your Bible, and list your own five reasons for that special request God has laid on your heart. Then go kneel before Him and plead your case.

CHAPTER NINE

A PLACE OF TAKING HOLD

You and I may take hold at any time upon the justice and the mercy
and the faithfulness and the wisdom,
the long suffering and the tenderness of God,
and we shall find there every attribute of the Most High to be,
as it were, a great battering ram with which we may open
the gates of heaven.
Charles Haddon Spurgeon

I often pray for children around the world on the basis of God's tenderness and compassion toward boys and girls. I claim His love, and hold fast to the promise of who He is.

Even a casual look at the life of Jesus in Scripture shows how these attributes of His character bubbled up like water from an artesian well every time He was around a child. It was as if He could hardly contain Himself from blessing them, drawing them near, and honoring them with a "first place" status in the kingdom. If that's the way He was with children who ran up to Him, boys and girls who could walk and see and hear and use their hands, how much more His heart must have gone out to handicapped children.

PLACE:
Orphanage #7,
Bucharest, Romania
TIME:
June 1991

It was good to cling to this picture of Jesus as I entered the

Bucharest orphanage. Especially when they carried little Vasile into the room to meet me.

They said he was seven or eight; he looked like a frail three-year-old. They told us he was dying of colon cancer. I looked at him...tiny hands and feet...faint little voice...soft brown eyes, clouded with pain. He seemed weak from lack of nutrition. When they lifted up his little shirt to show me his distended abdomen, he winced in pain.

I asked for Vasile to be sat in my lap.

"Vasile," I said, "Have you ever ridden a bicycle?"

"No."

"Would you like to go for a ride in my wheelchair? Da?"

He nodded.

"I'll share my wheels with you, Vasile!"

We wheeled around and around the drab, cement floored room as a steady rain pattered against the windows.

A small smile crossed his face. I made up a song as we wheeled around in the colorless little room. "Vasile is your name, Vasile is your name.

"Do you know Jesus, Vasile? Do you know where Jesus lives? He lives in heaven. Would you like to be with Him in heaven?"

Vasile nodded his little head.

I prayed, "Dear Jesus, we love You and we love how You love children. This little boy loves You, too. Take Him home to be with You, Jesus."

Mary Lance, one of our team's front-line, on-the-scene prayer warriors, prayed that if it was the Lord's will, that little Vasile might be healed.

I too, prayed silently with all my heart: *Lord, You had compassion on the little children when You walked on earth, and You are the same today...may these handicapped children have power with You, feel Your closeness...may You meet their needs as You met the needs of the boys and girls whom You blessed with Your own hands.*

We based our prayers on the power of God's attributes. And the Lord heard our petitions. Vasile was spared. He did not have colon cancer after all, but a treatable disease. Today he has a home and a family in Bakersfield, California. He is healthy and whole and full of little-boy mischief and smiles.

And he has his own bicycle.

TAKING HOLD OF HIS CHARACTER

In the early days of my paralysis I was desperate for a promise—any promise—that would bring hope into my dark and bleak world. Would I ever smile again? Would life have any meaning? Could anything good come from useless hands and feet?

A thin ray of hope broke through when a friend showed me a promise in the Bible that spoke about God's faithfulness. Philippians 1:6 told me to be confident that "he who began a good work in you will carry it on to completion until the day of Christ Jesus."

My friend encouraged me to take hold of that scripture, saying, "Joni, why don't you use that verse as a kind of 'lever.' Hold God to His Word. Believe He began a good work in you long before your accident. Why don't you contend, in prayer, that He will carry out that good work even though you're in a wheelchair?"

What my friend said made sense. My passport out of depression would be the faithfulness of God. Taking a grip on

His faithful character, I quoted Philippians 1:6 in prayer time and again—as though it were a lifeline. I didn't pray about it once, but many times, knocking and knocking at the door of His tenderness and mercy until He opened it.

Obviously, God needed no reminder of His faithfulness, but frankly, I believe He was delighted with my prayer. He enjoyed the fact that I took my prayer seriously, that I was ready to argue His faithfulness with Him and say, "Lord, You're the One who wrote that verse in Philippians, and I'm holding You to it. I know You're a promise-keeper because You say in Psalm 89 that You will never betray Your faithfulness. So I can say confidently that this is Your will: Carry to completion the good things You began in my life before my diving accident."

Being able to pray that way was a breath of fresh air. And you know what? I found peace. My depression was lifted. God was being faithful; He was keeping His promise.

HE CONTINUES A GOOD WORK

Oh, what a difference that prayer made. It was as though God pushed the fast-forward button on my walk with Him, and I began growing, as they say, by leaps and bounds. Out of nowhere, I began thirsting for His Word. Surprisingly, I was hungering after His righteousness. I began to see God "carrying to completion" His Son's life in me. My changed life, which was full of peace, patience, and joy, was a miraculous result of that simple prayer in which I took hold of the faithfulness of God.

Now what if I had not prayed that prayer? What if I had not been bold enough to remind God of His faithfulness as seen in Philippians 1:6? Would the Lord have continued to carry out

His good work in me? Sure, He would have—He's faithful to His promises whether I remind Him of them or not! But here's the point. I believe a special bond, a forged closeness, was custom-made between the Lord and me during those times of pleading in prayer. And who knows? Perhaps my life may not have changed as dramatically had I not spoken that prayer. Maybe God even speeded up the process!

HE CONTINUES A GOOD WORK IN YOU

I can imagine your thoughts: *This chapter is making me feel guilty. I can't pray that way.... I don't know enough Scripture to fill one sentence of a prayer. I'm too timid to pray using God's attributes anyway. I guess I've never seen the Lord work that way with me.*

If I've described you, if you think God will not "carry to completion" the good work He's begun in your life, then take comfort from this story:

Several years ago I was asked to record an album of songs. To get an idea of how the recording was done, I went down to the studio several days in advance just to listen to the rest of the musicians lay down the orchestral background music. Gathered in the little studio were some of the best musicians in Los Angeles: violinists and percussionists, guitar players, piano players, and all the rest.

When the arranger handed out the scores for a tune, these professionals would glance at it, rehearse it once, and go for a "take" to actually record. I was amazed they could play a very complicated score on sight. Most amazing of all, their efforts resulted in absolutely beautiful music.

But I was overwhelmed by what happened next. When the engineers in the booth played back the finished product, most of the musicians actually left the room! They took a break and milled around outside, sipping Cokes or coffee, oblivious to the beauty of the music they had just helped create. I couldn't believe it! How could they walk away and not want to hear how lovely the song sounded in its final form?

The musicians' interest in the music was dulled because they had recorded hundreds of other songs. What was so special about these? They did their jobs well, and they were finished.

Unlike those musicians, God doesn't walk away from His creation. His character is wrapped around His Word, just like the intertwining of His love and mercy in Philippians 1:6. That means that even though He has worked in thousands of lives, He doesn't take a break from His work in you. He's creating something beautiful in you, something far more lovely than a symphony of sound. For Him, it's not simply another job that needs to be done. His reputation is at stake and His Son's image is the model. It's perfection that God has in mind—maturity in Christ is the end result He seeks.

So please don't be fainthearted, thinking that your prayer life will never advance so far as to "take hold of the attributes of God." Don't give up…and don't think God gives up on you. He wants to carry to completion the work of prayer He has begun in your life. He's going to be around all the way until the day of Jesus Christ—to hear and see the dramatic impact of your prayers.

CONFIDENTLY CLAIM GOD'S ATTRIBUTES

Since God is so concerned with what He's doing in your life, you can confidently hold Him to His Word and claim His attributes in prayer. God enjoys it when we consciously seek His glory, His will, His character, and His heart in every situation.

Abraham prayed that way. When that old patriarch presented his case before God, he reminded the Lord, "Will not the Judge of all the earth do right?" (Genesis 18:25). Obviously God did not need to be reminded of His own justice. Abraham's prayer was persuasive because he pleaded, using God's character.

The prophet Habakkuk appealed to God's very nature in his prayer. It was a time of deep national distress for Judah. The ruthless Babylonian army was poised to sweep across the country like water from a ruptured dam. Yes, the prophet agreed with the Lord, Judah was deserving of His judgment. But how could God use a people even more evil than they as His rod of discipline?

> *Your eyes are too pure to look on evil; you cannot tolerate wrong.*
> *Why then do you tolerate the treacherous?*
> *Why are you silent while the wicked swallow up those more righteous than themselves?*
> (Habakkuk 1:13)

David pleaded God's character again and again. Discouraged by his own sins and unfaithfulness, he cried out:

> *Remember, O LORD, your great mercy and love, for they are from of old.*
> *Remeber not the sins of my youth an my rebellious ways; according to your love remember me, for you are good, O LORD.*
> (Psalm 25:6-7)

Does it sound a little cheeky to remind God of His attributes? Of His promises? Does it seem presumptuous? Yes, if you're the timid type. But remember, the Lord wants you to grow in prayer— even become a bold warrior in prayer.

How about it? Would you involve God in your prayer? If you're hurting or confused, find one of God's great attributes and, as Spurgeon says, use it "as...a great battering ram with which we may open the gates of heaven." Claim His love, plead His holiness, remind Him of His goodness, recount His longsuffering, present to Him His power, and pray His steadfastness. If you're remorseful and repentant over your sin, remind Him of His tender mercies. If you're in confusion, read to Him His own words about wisdom from Proverbs 4. If you're praying for your child, present your petition before the Lord, recounting to Him stories of how He blessed little children and delighted in them.

One final thought. The more you center in prayer on God's attributes, the more those attributes become a part of your life. Focus on God's mercies, and you will become merciful. Plead with Him His wisdom, and wisdom will be yours. Center your thoughts on His holiness, and you will grow in holiness. "But we all, with open face beholding as in a glass the glory of the Lord, are changed into the same image from glory to glory, even as by the Spirit of the Lord" (2 Corinthians 3:18, KJV).

Grab on to an attribute of God with all your heart and ask Him to deal with you accordingly. Humbly hold Him to His promises. God is delighted when you seek His will, His character, His glory—and yes, His heart—in your prayers.

Let's pause and enjoy God's attributes! Pray with me, saying:

My God, infinite is Thy might, boundless Thy love, limitless Thy grace, glorious Thy saving name. I ask great things of a great God. You are known, but beyond knowledge, revealed but unrevealed. You are the almighty Instructor; possess our minds with the grandeur of Thy perfections. Let us never forget Thy patience, wisdom, power, faithfulness, care, and never cease to respond to Thy invitations.
—(*Valley of Vision,* a collection of Puritan prayers and devotions.)

CHAPTER TEN

A PLACE OF PROMISE

*The sacred promises, though in themselves most sure and precious,
are of no avail for the comfort and sustenance of the soul
unless you grasp them by faith,
plead them by prayer, expect them by hope,
and receive them with gratitude.*

Charles Haddon Spurgeon

My father should have been raised as a cowboy out on the open plains. Actually, he almost was. Born in 1900, he led a rough-rider life, trading with the Indians in the Northwest, and scaling the highest peaks of the Rockies. I loved following in his footsteps, riding fast horses, hiking high mountains, and camping under the moon and stars. Dad was my hero.

PLACE:
*Manor Pines
Nursing Home
Fort Lauderdale,
Florida*

TIME:
May 1990

That's why it was so hard to face his ninetieth birthday. It was a day we had to celebrate at his bedside, as a series of strokes had left him severely debilitated. The family house in Maryland had been sold. Mother had moved her and Dad to Florida, where he resided in a cheery little nursing home. Mom walked from my uncle's house to the nursing home every morning to care for her husband's needs and then returned at night after he was put to bed.

Then, in a span of weeks, everything changed.

My father began to quickly fail. We knew that within days he was certain to pass away. At his bedside, we played inspirational music on a cassette recorder, sang hymns, prayed, and, most of all, read aloud promises from God's Word.

As the end drew near, we drew deep comfort from 1 Corinthians 15 and its ringing promises of death's ultimate defeat and new, wonderful bodies that will never, never die.

The body is "sown" in corruption; it is raised beyond the reach of corruption. It is "sown" in dishonor; it is raised in splendor. It is sown in weakness; it is raised in power. It is sown a natural body; it is raised a spiritual body...

For this perishable nature of ours must be wrapped in imperishability; these bodies which are mortal must be wrapped in immortality. So when the imperishable is lost in the imperishable, the mortal lost in the immortal, this saying will come true:

Death is swallowed up in victory.

For where now, O death, is your power to hurt us? Where now, O grave, is the victory you hoped to win...All thanks to God, then, who gives us the victory over these things through our Lord Jesus Christ! (1 Corinthians 15:42-44, 53-55,57, Phillips).

When you sit by the side of a loved one drawing his last ragged breaths on this world, those words become something more than nice-sounding phrases. They become the very ground under your feet, comforting you as you stand firm in that place of promise.

Lingering at my dad's bedside, we recalled other times and places where we, as a family, found comfort in the promises of God.

A lways an outdoorsman, Dad cultivated a love of the wild, wide-open places in all of us. Just a couple of years after my injury, our family took a month-long camping trip to Canada. We rented a Winnebago and drove deep into the province of Alberta, a beautiful part of the Rocky Mountains. We drove by glacier-scarred peaks, turquoise-blue rivers, and broad, alpine valleys. I sat by an open window, drinking in the sweet, crisp smell of pine air.

PLACE:
Canadian Rockies

TIME:
July 1971

We set up camp at Whistler's Mountain near Jasper, Alberta. Now, my family is the hardy, outdoor type. They love to hike, ride horses, and play tennis. So it didn't surprise me when Mom, Dad, and my sisters wanted to hike up the path to the towering cliffs above camp.

"I'll remain behind," I said.

I didn't want them to feel guilty about leaving me. I was as excited for them as if I were going myself. I would stay by the tent, read a book, and wait around until they returned.

After they threw on their backpacks, I watched them trek up the path. I was happy for them, but...I had mixed emotions. I found it difficult to sit there, and soon I felt tears welling up. I'm sure I could have used that time for a mountain-sized pity party, but instead, I decided to put the matter to prayer. I brought before God a promise of which I was certain.

I spoke aloud the promise of Philippians 4:6, "Be anxious about nothing, but present your requests to God and the peace of God will keep your heart and mind in Jesus."

A Place of Promise

And I began to pray.

"Lord," I said, "I know it is Your will for people to enjoy Your creation. That's why You've given us this beauty—the mountains, the trees, the streams. And Lord, I'm thankful for how beautiful and refreshing it all is to my heart. But God, I know You understand that I am human—You know all about my feelings right now.

"And so, as You told me to do in Philippians 4, I want to present my request to You: Please bring Your creation close to me, God. I can't get out into it, that's obvious, but I'm asking You to put me in touch with Your creation in a special way. And as You do, I take You at Your promise.... I believe You'll give me peace which transcends all understanding."

I offered that prayer, but I wasn't certain what avenue the Lord would take to answer it. I thought perhaps He would have a butterfly flit across my path or a caterpillar crawl across my knee. Anything to remind me of His presence and the closeness of His creation would have been fine.

Minutes passed—an hour in fact—and my interest returned to my book. Before long, my prayer slipped my mind. My family returned from their hiking trip, and as they slung off their backpacks, they told me all about their hike.

That night after dinner, Dad, my sister Kathy, and I sat around the campfire singing hymns. "Trust and obey, for there's no other way,..." we were harmonizing and having a good time. As we sang, though, I looked behind my sister, who was sitting across from me, and I saw what looked like a big black dog.

"Kathy, you'd better stop singing. There's something behind you."

She ignored me and started on the second verse.

"Wait a minute, that isn't a dog—*it's a black bear!* Kathy," I whispered hoarsely, "stop singing! There's a bear behind you!"

She just kept singing. "Trust and obey..."

"Kathy, stop singing! A BEAR is breathing down your neck!"

"There's no bear behind me," she laughed, but she stopped singing and turned around. Kathy and the bear locked eyes, then she froze, paralyzed with fear and excitement.

We sat very still and watched as the bear sniffed around Kathy's log, ambled over to me, and then sniffed my wheelchair. He smelled my foot pedals! He was sniffing the cuff of my jeans! I was so terrified, yet thrilled.

My sister, Jay, who was in the Winnebago washing dishes, heard the commotion, so she threw open the camper door and exclaimed, "Bear? Where?"

That panicked the bear. He whirled around, upset the Coleman stove, pots and pans, banged the picnic table, and galloped off into the night. My sisters scrambled for their cameras and ran after him.

As I lay in bed that night, I thought, *Wow, what a first-class answer to prayer!* This was no little butterfly or caterpillar. It was almost as if God, with His marvelous sense of humor, said, "You want to get closer to My creation? I'll get you so close to My creation, you'll never want to be that close again!"

The Lord had a reason for answering my prayer in such a big way. First, I'm sure He wanted to give me the peace He promised in Philippians 4:6—the verse I quoted to Him. But secondly, I believe God wanted to underscore a lesson. It was as if He said, "Now look, Joni, if I care enough about you to answer such a little request as, 'Bring Your creation close to me,' don't you think I am deeply concerned about the intimate details of your life that really matter? The loneliness, the heartache, the feelings of inferiority?"

As I lay in bed, I was filled with indescribable peace. The peace God had promised.

BELIEVE HIS PROMISES

You, too, can plead God's promises with certainty. Take God at His word. Believe His promises. Expect a great answer to prayer. God may not bring a bear to your front door, but the next time you present to God one of His promises, expect Him to keep it.

God is looking for men and women who will prove Him and His Word. There are no loopholes in His promises, and He delights in finding those people who will confirm the good things about His name and His Word through their suffering. God's promises are like a "crowbar to pry open" the storehouse of His grace.

In a way, God has given me the chance to do just that from this wheelchair. Over twenty-six years have passed since my diving accident, and I've had a few years of practice trying God's Word and proving His goodness and grace. If I were to sum it up, I would join with the psalmist in saying, "Your promises have been thoroughly tested, and your servant loves them" (Psalm 119:140).

What a change in attitude for me! There was a time when God's Word seemed burdensome. I could barely bring myself to give thanks in all things. It was drudgery to think that His grace was sufficient...if, indeed, that meant experiencing His grace from a wheelchair. It was hard to visualize how all things could possibly fit together into a pattern for good when I could not see any good in hands that were useless and legs that could not walk.

But now I hang Psalm 119:140 over my desk. I love God's promises because I have seen His Word work, and I have confidence His promises will see me through a lot more in the future.

It was through the trial of a broken neck that God proved in my life Romans 8:28: "And we know that in all things God works for the good of those who love him, who have been called according to his purpose." And His purpose is…making me more like Jesus. And that's good!

Think of it. Can you be one of those people through whom God delights to prove His promises? Have you viewed your suffering, however great or small, as a testing ground of Bible promises? If you have, I hope your heart will join with mine in saying, "Your promises have been thoroughly tested and Your servant loves them."

BE CERTAIN…BE SURE

We can plead God's promises with certainty. There's no need to doubt or second-guess when you pray. There's no need to scratch your head, unsure of what you're talking about. You can be *certain* of God's promises. It is this which will give you certainty in prayer. For instance, look at Solomon's prayer of dedication for the temple of Israel:

O LORD, God of Israel, there is no God like you in heaven…Now LORD, God of Israel, keep for your servant David my father the promises you made to him when you said, 'You shall never fail to have a man to sit before me on the throne of Israel, if only your sons are

A Place of Promise

careful in all they do to walk before me as you have done.' And now, O God of Israel, let your word that you promised your servant David my father come true (1 Kings 8:23,25-26).

Talk about being certain in prayer! Solomon had obviously made a spiritual diary of God's promises—the ones the Lord had given to David, his father—and took God at His word of honor. And don't you think God was delighted to fulfill that great promise in front of Solomon and His people? The Bible is replete with God's pledges and oaths, His vows and words of honor. And most of those promises God has given to you! Of course He would want you to be certain in prayer as you present to Him those promises.

YOUR QUIET PLACE...

People rely on different promises at different times and places in their lives. Select one of these prayers to help you where you are in your life today.

• A promise for peace: "You will keep him in perfect peace, whose mind is stayed on You, because he trusts in You" (Isaiah 26:3, NKJV).

• A promise for when you're depressed: "Therefore humble yourselves under the mighty hand of God, that He may exalt you in due time, casting all your care upon Him, for He cares for you" (1 Peter 5:6-7, NKJV).

• A promise for when you're tempted: "For in that He Himself has suffered, being tempted, He is able to aid those who are tempted" (Hebrews 2:18, NKJV).

• A promise for when you're impatient: "I waited patiently

for the LORD; and He inclined to me, and heard my cry" (Psalm 40:1, NKJV).

• A promise for when you're hurting: "Wait on the LORD; be of good courage, and He shall strengthen your heart; wait, I say, on the LORD! (Psalm 27:14, NKJV).

CHAPTER ELEVEN

A PLACE OF WORDLESS LONGING

When thou prayest, rather let thy heart be without words
than thy words without heart.
John Bunyan

The coastal mountains angle right into the ocean. A pebble beach, white sand. Small sycamore trees cluster at the crest of the beach.

Point Dume, a towering cliff, rises at the far end of the beach.

The rhythm of the waves matches the rhythm of your heart—slow, steady. Yet restless and surging. A pleasurable experience, everything touching your senses. But the waves, most of all, touch your *soul.*

PLACE:
Sycamore Cove
on the edge of the
Pacific Ocean
TIME:
June 1993

Our souls are restless. Raging and thirsting for fulfillment. For pleasure. We find ourselves in a place of wordless longing, always wanting more. And where we place our citizenship, whether in heaven or on earth, is revealed by those things we passionately desire. If we desire dull, sensual things of earth our souls reflect that dullness. But if our desires rise to find fulfillment in the exalted, in the noble, pure, and praiseworthy, then and only then do we find satisfaction, rich and pleasurable.

I'll be the first to admit that such longings heighten my loneliness here on earth. As a citizen of heaven, I know that I am destined for unlimited pleasure at the deepest level. I also know that nothing now quite meets the standards of my longing soul; and that quiet but throbbing ache within me drives me to anticipate heavenly glories above.

Will I miss Bridal Veil falls at Yosemite or the pleasurable taste of a charbroiled chicken Caesar salad? I doubt it. C. S. Lewis says, "Our natural experiences are like penciled lines on flat paper. If our natural experiences vanish in the risen life, they will vanish only as pencil lines vanish from the real landscape; not as a candle flame that is put out, but as a candle flame which becomes invisible because someone has pulled up the blind, thrown open the shutters, and let in the blaze of the risen sun."

Sometimes I get so homesick for heaven that the yearning swells like an ocean wave and I feel as if I'm being swept away, right then and there, to my better heavenly country. I learned long ago that spiritual growth will always include an awakening of these deep longings for heaven, for pleasure at its best. Such an awakening leads to the true contentment of asking less of this life because more is coming in the next.

That's why as a citizen of heaven, if I had a passport, I would copy this poem by William Herbert Carruth on the inside page:

Like tides on a crescent sea-beach, When the moon is new and thin,
Into our heart's high yearnings Come welling and surging in—

Come from the mystic ocean, Whose rim no foot has trod—
Some of us call it Longing, And others call it God.

Because God has placed powerful longings within you, it stands to reason that He must be the consummation of that need. He directs your longings toward heaven when He commands you to set your heart and mind where Christ is seated above.

At such times—when my prayer has found a place in heavenly glories above—I am at a loss for words. My prayer is more of a silent communion than a long-winded dissertation. Words are unnecesasry. Sentences only seem to clutter. My longings are best met when, in prayer, I simply let my heart beat in time with the Lord's.

WHEN WORDS AREN'T ENOUGH

It's not often I'm at a loss for words. But when I received a letter from a man named Steve and read his incredible story, I found myself sitting stunned and silent.

Steve, a narcotics agent, was paralyzed when shot in the neck four years earlier while on duty. He wrote, "I'm having a terrible time adjusting to my situation, and some words of inspiration would really come in handy right now."

I knew I had to telephone Steve and at least make an effort to share some words of encouragement he so desperately needed. On the phone, I realized Steve was breathing with the aid of a ventilator. He'd say a few words, then pause as his respirator pulled in air. He would then quickly finish his sentence, stopping again for another breath.

I've talked with lots of ventilator quadriplegics like Steve, and I don't find a respirator distracting, but I couldn't help but think, *No wonder this guy is having a terrible time adjusting. He's lost so much.*

I was at a loss for words. And I told Steve so. We agreed, though, that sometimes words aren't needed. He understood that, in a small way, I knew what he was going through. Before we hung up, I prayed with him. He was looking forward to an operation for a nerve implant in his neck so that he could at least breathe on his own. But even after that operation, he'll still have struggles. As he said in his letter, "Just existing is a hassle."

I'm touched that Steve understood my loss for words. Finding honest, concrete words of encouragement is impossible at times. But when I reread his letter, I thought of those words from Romans: "In the same way, the Spirit helps us in our weakness. We do not know what we ought to pray for, but the Spirit himself intercedes for us with groans that words cannot express" (Romans 8:26).

GOD UNDERSTANDS OUR GROANS

Immediately after church, a young woman with cerebral palsy approached me in her wheelchair.

CP is usually characterized by paralysis, weakness, or loss of coordination due to brain damage. Sometimes there are uncontrolled movements and slurred speech. This woman's speaking was especially difficult to grasp. She kept groaning a certain sentence over and over again. Even though I patiently asked her to repeat each word one by one, I still couldn't understand. The expression on her face gave me no clues at all. I couldn't tell if she was in terrible trouble or was simply trying to relay some profound experience.

Finally, after many attempts, I was able to piece her sentence together. She was asking me to help her find someone who could assist her to the restroom!

It was a simple request. But I felt so helpless, so inadequate that it had taken me so long to understand her. Once it dawned on me what she was requesting, I moved quickly to get her help!

Can you imagine the hardship of not being able to make your needs known? Wouldn't it be sad if there was no one around who could even understand your longings?

There are times when we want to talk to God...but somehow can't manage it. The frustration and pain and sense of loss go too deep. Fear locks our thoughts. Confusion scatters our words. Depression grips our emotions.

I'm so glad God can read my heart and understand what's going on even when I am handicapped by my own weakness for words. As it says in Hebrews 4:13, "Nothing...is hidden from God's sight. Everything is uncovered and laid bare before the eyes of him to whom we must give account."

Words are not always necessary. When we are in such trouble that we can't even find words—when we can only look toward heaven and groan in our spirit—isn't it good to remember that God knows exactly what's happening? The faintest whisper in our hearts is known to God. Even if it should be a sigh so faint that you are not even aware of it yourself, He has heard it. And not only heard it, but He *understands* it—right down to the slightest quiver registered in our innermost being.

You and I may certainly be handicapped when it comes to understanding the groans and sighs of one another. And others— yes, even those closest to us—may *never* be able to hear or interpret our deepest sorrows and longings.

A Place of Wordless Longing

But the One who searches hearts knows and understands. The Spirit is never handicapped by our weakness for words.

Our heavenward groans have a voice before God.

GOD WILL HELP YOU PRAY

Nobody is as "in touch" with our heart's longings as God. And when we are too weak to pray for ourselves, God finds words for us.

If you haven't noticed, Charles Spurgeon is one of my favorite writers, and I like how he describes God's action in our prayers:

It is a mark of wondrous condescension that God should not only answer our prayers when they are made, but should make our prayers for us. That the king should say to the petitioner, "Bring your case before me, and I will grant your desire," is kindness. But for him to say, "I will be your secretary. I will write out your petition for you. I will put it into proper words so that your petition shall be framed acceptably," this is goodness at its utmost stretch. But this is precisely what the Holy Ghost does for us poor, ignorant, wavering, weak men. Jesus in His agony was strengthened by an angel; you are to be helped by God Himself. Aaron and Hur held up the hands of Moses, but the Holy Ghost Himself helps your infirmities.

LIKE A FATHER, HE LISTENS

There is nothing that moves a loving father's soul quite like his child's cry. What loving parent can resist the cry of his or her baby? In Psalm 5:1-2 David opens his prayer by saying, "Give ear to my words, O LORD, consider my sighing. Listen to my cry for help, my King and my God, for to you I pray."

Up to his ears in trouble, his heart pounding in fear, David wanted God to hear his cry.

Sound familiar to you parents? Of all people, you should understand how precious to God are the cries of His children. If your baby is upstairs in his crib and he cries, instantly you know what's wrong. You can tell from the sound of his cry whether he's grumpy, waking up, hungry, or hurt. A baby, unable to speak, can tell his parents many things simply by the sound of his cry.

Someone once said that prayer is the child's helpless cry to the Father's attentive ear. When our prayer goes up like a cry, God knows exactly what our need is. He can tell if our cry is an urgent prayer for help or a sighing prayer of discouragement. Maybe it's a heartwarming prayer of gratitude. Much like a mother or father with a child, God heeds the voice of our crying.

And remember, God does more than hear words—He reads hearts. David said, "O LORD, consider my sighing." Hearts sigh. And our Father delights in listening for those whispers of sighing which tell Him our heart needs help.

WHEN WE DON'T KNOW HOW TO PRAY FOR OTHERS

Our work at JAF Ministries is an outreach to those with disabilities, such as cerebral palsy, mental retardation, spinal cord injuries, muscular dystrophy, or multiple sclerosis. When I pray for these people, I remind God of the way Christ's heart was touched with compassion, not pity, when He met blind persons. When He met those who were deaf or paralyzed, He was moved with love.

I'm sure many of these people were unable to put into words all that they felt when they met the Lord Jesus. But He ministered

A Place of Wordless Longing

to each unspoken request; He touched them with His love even when they didn't say a word.

And that's exactly how I prayed for Steve, my ventilator-dependent friend in a wheelchair. I may not have known how to decipher the slightest quiver in his hurting heart, but I knew that God understood; God could meet those needs.

So when I pray for the people involved with our ministry, I remind God that people need His love now just as much as they did when Jesus walked on the earth. I plead the sorrows of God's people and remind the Father that Jesus dealt with individuals who were torn apart by heartache and loneliness. I remind the Father of Christ's compassion for those who are lost and confused. Even though I don't know the specific burdens my fellow Christians are bearing, God does.

YOUR QUIET PLACE...

Reach back in your mind and recall the most meaningful times when a dear friend comforted you through your hurt. You may not have been able to express your heartache, but remember how your friend held you? Looked into your eyes? Cried with you? Do you recall special words that fit the need for the moment? Doesn't that memory warm your heart?

Now—transfer that remembrance to your relationship with your heavenly Father. Imagine for a moment His compassion when He hears the groaning you're too weak to even utter. Think of how instant He is in responding to your cry. While the memory is still in your mind, talk with Him now—straight from your heart.

A Quiet Place in a Crazy World

CHAPTER TWELVE

A PLACE OF JESUS' NAME

~~~

Like others, I have prayed for healings, for miracles, for guidance, and for assistance. Frankly, there were times I was sure God would answer me because I had mustered strong feelings of faith. But many of those times nothing happened—or if it did, it was entirely unlike what I had anticipated.... The fact is that my prayer life cannot be directly tied to the results I expect or demand. I have had many opportunities by now to see that the things I want God to do in response to my prayers can be unhealthy for me. I have begun to see that worship and intercession are far more the business of aligning myself with God's purposes than asking Him to align with mine.

Gordon Macdonald

How many adjectives do you need to describe Manila? Hot, steamy, sweaty, noisy, polluted, crowded. Yes. All these and more.

A converted jeep-bus carried us bumping and jolting over muddy highways of half-dirt and half crumbled asphalt to a residential home for disabled orphans on the outskirts of the city.

The House with No Steps—so named because of its accessible ramps—is at the end of a side street off the highway, past an abandoned gas station

> PLACE:
> *"The House with No Steps,"*
> *Manila, the Philippines*
>
> TIME:
> *Summer 1989*

overgrown with vines and banana trees, a few crowded shacks, and countless barking mongrel dogs.

The Catholic-administered house is like a quiet oasis in the middle of poverty and despair. Neatly trimmed lawns. Flowers. A scattering of rusty, but well-maintained out buildings.

As our bus pulled up into the drive, children scurried from all sides of the little compound to greet us—kids on crutches, clinging to walkers, or racing along in their wheelchairs. One little boy, Nehru Paunil, endeared himself to us. He looked just like photos of my husband, Ken, when he was a little boy.

Over the years, many people from all over the world have visited this place and prayed over these little ones for healing in Jesus' name. The nuns told us that the visitors have brought holy water or handkerchiefs blessed by the Pope himself. And nothing happened—or so they thought. Many of these compassionate foreigners have gone home disappointed and dismayed that they weren't able to do something for these precious children that they pitied.

And yet the children *have* experienced healing, but perhaps not the kind the foreign visitors had in mind. You've never seen a more happy, smiling, laughing group of children. They wear clean, starched clothes. Their home is as spic and span as it could possibly be. And they are loved dearly. The miracle, obviously, is their attitude toward life and their disabilities…their great joy.

What does it mean, then, to "pray in Jesus' name"? Some kind of blank check that heaven is always obliged to cover? What does it mean to pray in the power of His name?

I have come to understand that praying in His name means praying for things that are consistent with *His character*, with who He is. Somehow, we've distorted it to mean that Jesus is obliged to see to our constant comfort, financial prosperity, or physical healing.

A CARTE BLANCHE?

"In Jesus' name…be healed!"

Lying in bed, totally paralyzed, you can imagine how words like these voiced by a television preacher intrigued me. More than just being interested in the words of a faith healer, I was also interested in what the Bible had to say about healing. I desperately wanted out of my wheelchair!

When I studied the Bible, I was impressed that Jesus never passed over anyone who needed healing. He opened the eyes of the blind and the ears of the deaf and even raised up the paralyzed.

I was also impressed with a number of Scripture passages that seemed to indicate that I could ask whatever would be in God's will and Jesus would do it. A request for healing seemed consistent with His will, and one of my favorite passages was John 16:23-24: "My Father will give you whatever you ask in my name. Until now you have not asked for anything in my name. Ask and you will receive, and your joy will be complete."

So I began to pray for healing in Jesus' name. I used examples from the past of God's great provision for others. "Jesus Christ is the same yesterday and today and forever," I reminded God (Hebrews 13:8). "And Jesus healed back then. That means He can heal right now. So Lord, that You might receive glory, lift me up."

In order to show genuine faith, I called my friends on the telephone and said, "Hey, you guys, next time you see me I'm going to be standing on my feet." I even went to a couple of "faith healing" services. I was convinced that my healing was in God's plan and that He would raise me up to bring more glory to Himself. And praying it all in Jesus' name seemed to put the seal on my destiny.

But nothing happened. Days, weeks passed, and I would look at my arms and legs as though they were separate from me, and think, "You're healed, body!" For some reason, my fingers and my feet didn't get the message. My mind said, "Move!"

But nothing happened.

GOD'S ANSWER TO PRAYER

I couldn't understand. Didn't God's Word promise I could ask for anything in Jesus' name and it would be granted so that my joy would be complete? Surely God knew it would overjoy me to be healed.

I thought perhaps I wasn't searching the Scriptures thoroughly enough. It was then God led me back to Hebrews, the same book in which I found that marvelous verse about His being the same yesterday, today, and forever.

In the eleventh chapter of Hebrews, I found that roll call of great heroes of the faith—seventeen men and women who, because of their God-honoring and God-pleasing faith, experienced miracles. People like Noah, Abraham, Isaac, Jacob, Joseph, and others. These people conquered kingdoms, gained what was promised, shut the mouths of lions, escaped the edge of the sword, and received the dead back to life.

But then I noticed an interesting change initiated by two little words in verse 35: "and others." Others were tortured some faced jeers and floggings. Others were chained and put in prison. They were stoned. These saints had just as much God-honoring and God-pleasing faith as those named earlier in the chapter—but they did not receive miracles.

I realized I was probably among those who had faith, yet also a lifetime of hard knocks and trials. I was comforted by Hebrews 11:39-40: "These were all commended for their faith, yet none of them received what had been promised. God had planned something better for us so that only together with us would they be made perfect."

God had a better plan for me. I began to see my healing was not physical, but spiritual. Through that search I learned more about God, which is really what most of His answers to prayer are about anyway. I learned that Jesus is the same yesterday, today, and forever: always just, always holy, always full of love, always sensitive, always long-suffering. He never has, and never will, change.

PRAYING IN JESUS' NAME

But *what about* that promise in John 16:24? "Until now," Jesus told His followers, "you have not asked for anything in my name. Ask and you will receive, and your joy will be complete."

What was that, if it wasn't some kind of guarantee?

I assumed all along, of course, that it had to be God's will to put me back on my feet. But God's will obviously meant something bigger and, yes, even better. It's taken me years to understand, but the deep and enduring joy I have has far outlived whatever immediate joy I would have experienced had I been healed. It's all because I've finally learned what it means to pray in Jesus' name.

Praying in Christ's name means to pray in a manner consistent with His life...with who He is...and the kinds of things

He thinks are important. From the life of Jesus we find good examples for the sorts of requests we might include in our prayers.

We assume that it is God's will for us to have pure and polished reputations, but look at Jesus—He was slandered and mocked. Despised and snubbed. And as far as His reputation was concerned, He was lampooned as the national laughing stock.

We think it's God's will for us to have a new and bigger house, but Jesus, during the height of His ministry, never had a real home or even a place to lay His head. He hung His sandals and staff in the homes of friends, the bows of boats, and even moonlit fields behind villages.

We're convinced words such as suffering and disappointment shouldn't be included in the Christian's vocabulary, but Jesus was a man of sorrows, acquainted with grief.

Turning His back on ease and comfort, Jesus opted for the school of suffering (Hebrews 5:8) which rewarded Him with the things He really prized: peace and patience, self-control and longsuffering, gentleness and sensitivity.

Should we, His servants, expect a life easier than our Master?

I don't think so. When we pray in Jesus' name, we should expect to receive things consistent with that name, such as patience and long-suffering. We might pray for financial prosperity, a new career, success with the opposite sex, or physical healing, but God may choose to give us something even more precious, something even closer to what His name and character are all about.

His presence.

His perspective.

His endurance.

His deep and lingering peace in the midst of turmoil and pain and loneliness and disappointment.

And that's what I've gained from praying for healing in Jesus' name. No, I don't have a repaired physical body, but I have more joy and peace than two strong legs and two nimble hands could *ever* have brought me.

MORE ABOUT PRAYING IN HIS NAME

Take another look at John 16:23, "...my Father will give you whatever you ask in my name." When Jesus shared these words with His disciples, He was giving them a new perspective on how to have their needs met. He was teaching them how to seek. When we read, "my Father will give you," what more could we wish for than to have what God desires to give us? Remember, "No good thing does he withhold from those whose walk is blameless" (Psalm 84:11). And don't forget James 1:17: "Every good and perfect gift is from above, coming down from the Father of the heavenly lights."

When we ask "in His name," we ask for everything Christ purchased and promised through His death and resurrection. And to what has His death given us access? The Lord "has blessed us in the heavenly realms with every spiritual blessing in Christ" (Ephesians 1:3). When we pray in His name, we can be sure of this answer: God will bless us with every spiritual blessing. Now that's a big answer to prayer!

And look at John 16:24: "Until now you have not asked for anything in my name." Up until this point, His disciples had asked nothing in comparison to what was now ready to be poured out upon them. The Lord, by His death and resurrection, was ready to pour out His Spirit and give larger gifts than anyone realized. Perhaps the disciples had prayed before, but never had they prayed in the name of Christ and all that His name offered them.

"Ask and you will receive, and your joy will be complete" (John 16:24). Finally, when you think about it, isn't joy what you ultimately desire, whatever your petition? Whether you ask for yourself or on behalf of a friend, aren't you really looking for joy? Well, joy is promised. Joy is one of those spiritual blessings God is ready to pour out upon you. We are told to aim high in prayer, to expect to receive joy. Fullness of joy is ours as we pray without ceasing. "Be joyful always; pray continually" (1 Thessalonians 5:16-17).

And that is one answer to prayer that will always be a resounding "Yes!" Whatever your circumstances, God wants to give you joy. It's the highest and greatest result of praying in His name.

YOUR QUIET PLACE...

When the Lord invited His followers to go to the Father in His name, He was talking about a brand-new relationship. Previously, men and women approached God with caution and fear through the priests. But since the resurrection of Jesus, all believers can talk to God...directly...anytime we want. To get a clear idea of what it means to go to God "in Jesus' name," let's personalize, as a prayer, John 15. Say it with me now:

Jesus, You are the vine and our Father is the gardener... I am already clean because of the word You have spoken to me. I remain in You and You remain in me because I, as the branch, can bear no fruit by myself; I must remain in You, the vine.... Apart from You, I can do nothing. As Your words remain in me and I remain in You, I may ask from You, and You will give to me so that You will receive glory. And this is Your glory—that I bear much fruit, showing myself to be Your disciple. In Your name, Amen.

What a way to pray—use Scripture and personalize it!

CHAPTER THIRTEEN

A PLACE OF PRAISE

———

Let praise—say not merely thanksgiving,
but praise—always form an ingredient of thy prayers.
We thank God for what He is to us;
for the benefits which He confers;
and the blessings with which He visits us.
But we praise Him for what He is in Himself,
for His glorious excellences and perfections,
independently of their bearing on the welfare of the creature.
Edward M. Goulburn

E cuador is a spiritually dark country. Quito, the capitol, with all its urban blight and decay, is, if possible, darker still.

Of all the corners of the world I've visited, this was the most oppressive. A heavy, brooding fog of spiritual menace clings to this remote, mountaintop city. Undercurrents of Catholicism-gone-awry, animism, spiritism, witchcraft, and mountain magic come-down-from-the-Andes meet and mingle in its somber streets and anguished slums.

PLACE:
Quito, Ecuador
TIME:
November 1991

The air smells forever of burnt mountain coffee, cheap wine, and the smoke of marijuana and bad cigars. On the street corners, Indian children play in the gutters. Their mothers squat by small fires, cooking tortillas, or stand on the corners selling their handmade blankets. The Indian women look old before their time. Weary. Vacant-eyed. Abused. Bent. Beaten down. The children are skilled in everything from begging to pick-pocketing.

In Quito, we were at fourteen thousand feet above sea level—as high as the peak of California's towering Mount Shasta. And yet even at that altitude, we could look behind us and see other mountains soaring higher and higher into the thin air. That's how high the Andes are—and how isolated.

One of our meetings was at a sports center. As we drove our jeep through the dark streets, I could only guess at what the huddles of men on the street corners were dealing out of their pockets. Their laughter sounded hard and harsh, without mirth or joy.

We got out of our jeep and I wheeled along the cracked sidewalk past discarded wine bottles and sleeping Indians on cardboard mats. The stench of urine and rotting garbage drifted through the alley ways.

In the sports center, dirty and dimly lit, we held our rally. Looking out into the crowd, I noticed a mother who carried her spina bifida boy in a large bandanna knotted around her head. A missionary sang with a group of Indian girls from a Christian school. The girls, smiling and shy, dressed in colorful *serapes*, accompanied their songs with native instruments. A team of boys in wheelchairs gave a basketball demonstration. An Ecuadorian pastor gave a simple, heart-felt gospel message, and then I sang.

Somehow, that shabby, dim little gymnasium blossomed with transcendent beauty.

It was a place of light and praise, a place of God's presence.

It brimmed with His Word, and with sweet songs of praise. The hope and joy and laughter spilled out into the street. Praise seemed all the more powerful and glorious in contrast to the surrounding darkness. It was like a delicate flower growing out of a cesspool. It was an island of joyful light and sanity and reason in a churning sea of cruelty, injustice, and suffering.

A quiet place in a crazy world.

Praise, I've discovered, has the power to transform its setting—wherever that may be.

THE PRAISE OF A DETERMINED HEART

It's not often I casually flip through a book like Numbers, but the other day I came across an interesting story in chapter 21.

I read about the Israelites as they journeyed through the desert near the borders of Moab (Numbers 21:10ff.). Not a fun place, the desert. They were thirsty. The Israelites had one thought in their minds: *We need water, but we don't want snakes.* The last time they needed water they had complained against God, and God had sent venomous snakes in response (Numbers 21:5-9).

They had learned a painful lesson. This time they decided not to panic. No complaints. Instead, they praised. And God, in response, gave them water—a real miracle in a wilderness desert and a striking example of how God will refresh His saints when they praise Him.

I'm not unlike the Israelites—it's taken me awhile to learn that praise is the answer. There have been dry and dusty days in my soul, sometimes a coldness in my spirit. A cloud of gloom will hang heavily over me and no matter what I do or who I see, everything is an effort. At times like these, it's easy to complain.

As far as Satan is concerned, complaints and grumbling "make his day." Satan claps his hands in glee when we wander in a dry and lifeless wilderness. One of his goals is to force complaints from the children of God and render useless our labor for the Lord. But there is a way out of that spiritual stalemate, and the answer is found in Numbers 21.

Praise the Lord. I don't mean that flippantly or superficially, and I'm not talking about a mechanical exercise, either. I mean praise that is sincere, even if you have to grit your teeth and voice psalms of worship when your heart's not in it. Meaningful praise is sometimes praise you don't even feel. At least, not right away.

Even David the psalmist occasionally approached praise that way. You can almost hear him speak with a clenched jaw when he says in Psalm 57:7, "My heart is fixed, O God, my heart is fixed: I will sing and give praise" (KJV). You see, a fixed heart is a determined heart. David's heart was locked into trusting God and His sovereignty despite the difficulties.

And if you're hurting, Jesus stands ready to help you give praise. It says in Isaiah 61 that "He has sent me to bind up the brokenhearted...to bestow on them a crown of beauty instead of ashes, the oil of gladness instead of mourning, and *a garment of praise instead of a spirit of despair.*" Do you see? Sometimes praise—like a garment that's not even a part of you—has to be pulled on over your heavy spirit.

You've been there before—the heavy sighing, the pain of even praying, let alone praising. You can take a giant step forward on your spiritual journey, straight out of the dry and barren desert, if you are able to say with the psalmist, "Why are you downcast, O my soul? Why so disturbed within me? Put your hope in God, for *I will yet praise him, my Savior and my God*" (Psalm 42:5).

TEACH US TO PRAISE

Who, what, where, how, when, and *why.* Remember those words? Every time you opened your high school textbook to study, those words were your guide. If you could learn who did what, where, to whom, how, and why, you probably understood your subject.

It's no different when it comes to praising God. It's not something that comes naturally to any of us. Praise runs an aggravating interference pattern against our nature. It goes against our grain. Occasionally, praise feels more like a duty, an obligatory lip service performed at the opening of our prayers.

But remember David's words in Psalm 57:7, "My heart is fixed, O God, my heart is fixed; I will sing and give praise" (KJV). I like David's words, "I will." The psalmist refocused his emotions and realigned his thoughts by redirecting his will to praise. David taught himself that praise was good for his soul, as well as glorifying to God.

So *who* is to praise God? I am! You are! And not only us, but all of creation gets involved: "You will go out in joy and be led forth in peace; the mountains and hills will burst into song before you, and all the trees of the field will clap their hands" (Isaiah 55:12). And as someone has said, why should the trees have all the fun? Praise is befitting for God's people.

Where do we praise God? The psalms tell us to praise God "among the nations" and "among all peoples" (Psalm 96:3). Praise is fitting wherever we are—humming a praise song at the stoplight, quoting a favorite praise verse while you're folding laundry, repeating the words of a hymn of praise when you're gardening.

How do we praise God? With our mouths, with voices of joy, "with the psaltery," and with great shouts (Psalms 33:1-3; 63:5). The Bible says we can even praise God with "tambourine and dancing...with the strings and flute" (Psalm 150:4). I have a favorite album of instrumental music I've virtually memorized, and I love praising God in all the places where the melodies rise or the tunes become soft and gentle.

When do we do all this? Look at Psalm 34:1: "I will extol the LORD at all times." That's rather encompassing, isn't it? Other psalms tell us that we are to praise God all day long, continually, or seven times a day (Psalms 35:28; 71:6; 119:164). I think one of the most meaningful times to praise God is when I wake up in the middle of the night and can't go back to sleep. It's comforting and reassuring to praise God "through the watches of the night" (Psalm 63:6).

Finally, *what* do we give praise for? Well, at least one psalm goes on for pages praising God for His mighty acts (Psalm 105). Elsewhere, we learn to praise God for His name, His Word, His mighty power, His wonders, and His faithfulness, to mention a few (Psalms 8:1; 56:4; 66:3; 89:5; 119:105). Perhaps Psalm 150:2 sums it up best: "Praise him for his surpassing greatness."

Why do we praise God? Romans 8:32 says it all: "He who did not spare his own Son, but gave him up for us all—how will he not also, along with him, graciously give us all things?" No wonder the heavenly choir sings, "Worthy is the Lamb, who was slain, to receive power and wealth and wisdom and strength and honor and glory and praise!" (Revelation 5:12). We praise God because He is worthy of our praise.

WE HAVE NO REASON TO FEAR GOD

Still, you may not consider yourself a good pupil of praise. If so, let me see if I can put my finger on the reason why: Of the Trinity, whom do you relate to best? God the Father, Jesus the Son, or the Holy Spirit?

I know what you're thinking: *It's a trick question—they're all the same!* You're right, but I know many of us relate to the different Persons in the Trinity in very different ways.

I heard of a woman, for example, who was terrified of God the Father. She read all about Him in the Old Testament, how He commanded His leaders to destroy entire towns, how He slammed down an angry fist against sin, how He demanded a high and holy standard. She couldn't relate to God the Father, much less praise Him.

But, she said, she could praise Jesus. She more easily related to Him. Jesus spent time reaching out to the hurting; He talked to handicapped people at the temple; He took a few minutes to chat with children; and He was always on the look-out for the underdog. Jesus was sensitive, kind, and compassionate—and this woman felt drawn to God the Son. She sensed no condemnation from Him, even when she stumbled and fell into sin. This woman prayed solely to Jesus—she opened all her conversations with God with the name of the Lord Jesus.

But then something amazing happened.

She read the first chapter of Hebrews and learned that Jesus is the exact representation of God. She noticed a cross reference and flipped over to John 1:18: "No one has ever seen God, but God the One and Only, who is at the Father's side, has made him known."

A Place of Praise

The woman was fascinated. She then realized that knowing Jesus was the same as knowing the Father. She had no reason to fear or tremble. She could relate to God the Father because He and the Son are one in the same.

Maybe in the Old Testament people were afraid to approach God, but Jesus threw wide open the door of access to the Father, and that alone should cause us to praise. What freedom. What confidence. We have no reason to fear and every reason to trust Him and give Him adoration and worship.

WHEN WE CAN'T SAY ENOUGH

Have you ever been so filled, so overflowing with praise that you could hardly stop? David had that happen: "My mouth is filled with your praise, declaring your splendor all day long" (Psalm 71:8). Have you ever been in a position where you simply couldn't say enough good things about God?

When I wrote my third book, *Choices...Changes,* a good chunk of chapters was devoted to my husband, Ken. As I work on my books, sometimes I use my computer with my mouthstick, but most of the time I have to borrow other people's hands. One day my secretary sat next to me typing a mile a minute as I talked a mile a minute about Ken. How he looked the first time I saw him...how he talked...how he smiled...how he carried himself...how he moved when he played racquetball. The words about our dating flowed effortlessly. Writing about our wedding day and marriage was pure joy. Obviously, I didn't need a Thesaurus to think of adjectives. I wanted to go on and on.

And sometimes I did! My secretary would have to say, "Uh, Joni, don't you think you've talked enough about Ken's muscles?"

Or, "Joni, that's the fourth time in this chapter you've told us how handsome Ken is."

Isn't that funny? I just couldn't say enough good stuff about my husband.

I'll bet it's the same with those you love, too. You want others to know how special that person is—whether it's your mate, your friend, your child, your niece, your nephew, or your grandchild. The best part is finding someone genuinely interested in *listening* to your glowing descriptions. It actually multiplies your pleasure.

Listen in as the author of Hebrews talks about his best Friend, Jesus. It's as if someone had approached him and said, "You seem to put a great deal of stock in this Person, Jesus Christ. Just who is He, anyway? Why are you so excited about Him? Can you describe Him?"

Could He ever! Finding a listening ear, the writer can't say enough. Look at the passage beginning in Hebrews 1:1:

In the past God spoke to our forefathers through the prophets at many times and in various ways, but in these last days he has spoken to us by his Son, whom he appointed heir of all things, and through whom he made the universe. The Son is the radiance of God's glory and the exact representation of his being, sustaining all things by his powerful word. After he had provided purification for sins, he sat down at the right hand of the Majesty in heaven. So he became as much superior to the angels as the name he has inherited is superior to theirs.

Just glancing through this list gives us more than enough reasons to praise the Lord. Notice the six "reasons to praise":

• Christ is the appointed heir of all creation. Right from the beginning, the writer lifts Jesus up to where He belongs.

• It was through the spoken word of Jesus that the universe was made. Look around you. Everything from mountains to mulberry bushes was given life by the Lord Jesus.

• The Son is the radiance of God's glory. Just as the brilliance of the sun cannot be separated from the sun itself, Jesus can't be separated from the glory of the Father—He is God Himself.

• Jesus is the exact representation of the Father's being. Just as a stamp will leave its impression on warm wax, Jesus is the *exact* representation of the character and nature of God.

• Jesus is "sustaining all things by his powerful word" (1:3). Just as He created the world by the Word of His mouth, He is holding together all that has been created. What power!

• Jesus provided purification for sins—His wonderful work on the cross. By His death, Christ paid the huge penalty for our sins so that God's justice was satisfied. Jesus "sat down at the right hand of the Majesty in heaven" (1:3). His work of redemption completed, Jesus returned to His place by His Father's side. It is from His Father's throne that Jesus now rules over all.

With the ink flowing fast on his parchment, the excited writer goes on and on. Chapter one, chapter two, chapter three, chapter four...Jesus, Jesus, Jesus, Jesus.

How is it with you? If someone asked you to list a few descriptive phrases about the Lord Jesus, would the words fall effortlessly from your mouth, or would you scramble for *Roget's Thesaurus* for extra adjectives and adverbs?

If you find that you don't have enough adjectives to describe Him, I'd like to introduce you to the author of Hebrews. Sorry I can't give you his name, but he got so wrapped up in his

Subject he forgot to introduce himself. Maybe the two of you can get away together for a few minutes today.

There's nothing an excited writer would love more than a listening ear.

YOUR QUIET PLACE...

Our mouths can be filled with His praises! And everywhere we go can be a place of praise.

What has your mouth been full of so far today? Scolding? Nit-picking? Quibbling? Pause now and fix your heart on praise to God. Consider the who, where, why, and when of your praise. Speaking of when, why not right now?

If you have a thesaurus on your bookshelf (if not, a dictionary will do), look up words such as *noble* and *great* and *honor* and *praise.* Jot down synonyms so that you fill an entire page. Now you have plenty of language to praise the Lord.

CHAPTER FOURTEEN

A PLACE OF SACRIFICE

Let us continually offer to God a sacrifice of praise—the fruit of lips that confess his name
(Hebrews 13:15).

Neither will I offer burnt offerings unto the LORD my God of that which doth cost me nothing
(2 Sanuel 24:24, KJV).

E verywhere we go in Poland, people give us flowers. Fresh, thick bouquets of friesians and sweet peas. Tulips and gladiola in full bloom in our drab hotel rooms.

But how odd it is to see these same flowers swishing in the wind. Here. Here in Auschwitz. Even though the grounds of this death camp are so very tidy, delicate wisps of wildflowers crop up here and there, around the bases of brick buildings and trunks of trees. We wonder if the government,

PLACE:
Auschwitz, Poland

TIME:
April 1982

which operates a museum here, has sown wildflower seeds to brighten this horrible, depressing place.

I notice a row of lovely rose bushes planted just yards away from the gruesome gas chambers. I ask our guide about the roses, and he is quick to point out that where flowers are now was once hard, naked clay, every blade of grass picked clean by starving prisoners.

Bare bricks and barbed wire...storehouses of eyeglasses and hair and gold teeth, canes and crutches, shoes, hearing aids...stacks of yellowed and dusty record books, neatly tabulated names and numbers...gallows and guard towers...even the ominous chimneys and the ovens—all these things I've always associated with Nazi death camps are here.

I shiver, but not from the cold. To think that handicapped people like me were the first to be exterminated, labeled as "useless bread gobblers."

But even this thought is not entirely new.

It's the flowers. The flowers are something I didn't expect. And for that reason, their out-of-placeness touches me as nothing else.

We journey the short distance from Auschwitz to Birkenau. Here, trainloads of Jews and dissidents were emptied out into the freezing night to face the machine guns of powerful and insane men. Children were gun-butted one way; their mothers herded the other. Men were separated into groups of the old and young. But virtually all of them, millions of them, ended up in one place—the incinerator, now crumbled and overgrown at the end of the camp.

A crazy world, yes.

Nothing stands in this camp. Our guide explains that what appear to be orderly rows of heaps of brick were once the smoke stacks of wooden barracks. Nothing remains of the guard towers. Even the train tracks and railroad ties are rotted and uprooted.

But light, airy little field daisies carpet the acres, swaying in wave upon wave.

"What are you thinking?" Ken asks, stooping to pluck a wildflower.

"I was thinking of Tante Corrie...Corrie ten Boom," I finally answer. "She was in a place not unlike this." I nod toward the field of ghosts. "By all accounts, she should have died forty years ago in that concentration camp," I sigh.

Ken shakes his head in wonder. "Who would have thought she would leave that awful place. At fifty years of age," he marvels, his eyes fastened on the crumbled incinerators just yards away. "And then to start a whole new ministry."

I recall Tante Corrie's funeral at a small suburban cemetery just a few miles south of Los Angeles. It was the flowers that impressed me that day, too. No hothouse blooms stuck in styro-foam cut-out shapes of hearts or crosses or doves. No white satin banners with gold-sprinkled messages of sympathy. Instead, there were vases—tens of vases—of freshly cut tulips of yellow and red. Bouquets of dewy white carnations and bunches of heavy red roses someone had clipped from Corrie's backyard.

The casket was closed. The music was Bach. The eulogies were glowing but understated. The only extravagance was the profusion of flowers. The little stone chapel was filled with a sweet fragrance.

Now I sit in silence in this vast field, memories of Corrie stirring my thoughts. The only things that move are the wind and the daisies. It is at once striking and poignant. For Corrie, who came out of this pit of this hell, would be the first to say that the suffering in that place confronted her with the reality of the love or hate in her own heart. The confinement of her lonely cell attacked her own vanity and lonely pride. The crushing needs of her fellow prisoners constantly exposed her own need to give and share. She could not blame. She could only forgive.

It was a sacrifice of praise to the One who had sacrificed everything for us.

I drop my gaze down to the daisies Ken has tucked into the straps of my arm splints. A knowing smile crosses my lips. I would be the first to say that my wheelchair confronts me daily with the love or hate in my own heart. It attacks my pride and constantly exposes my need to give to others who suffer. I have no one to blame for my circumstances.

I glance at Ken who sits beside me in the grass. God has placed us together to have and to hold. To build up. To encourage. To love. Our marriage tirelessly exposes my need…our need to give and share and to cast aside blame. Our need to sacrifice for each other, and for our Lord.

A SACRIFICE OF PRAISE

Sacrifice. Sound foreboding? A little off-putting?

To clear up the meaning of that word, my dictionary says that sacrifice is "a giving up of something valued for the sake of something else." When we sacrifice, it costs us, doesn't it?

That helps define for us "sacrifice of praise." If you praise the Lord through a minor hardship or a major trial, you are offering a sacrifice of praise. Such a sacrifice costs you plenty—your pride, your anger, your human logic, and the luxury of your complaining tongue. A sacrifice of praise costs you your will, your resentment, and even your desire to have your own way in a situation. And for whose' sake do we give up these things? We do so for the sake of Christ and for His glory.

Whether it's a financial crunch, a sudden illness, or a personal defeat, if you fix your heart on praise to God, then you have offered a sacrifice. If you've ever cried during those heartbreaking difficulties, "Lord, I will hope in You and praise You more and more," then you know you have offered words which have cost you plenty. Praise in those circumstances is painful. Nevertheless, it is logical, even if our logic argues that God has no idea what He's doing.

Often, we assume that praise must be a bubbly explosion of enthusiastic phrases, happy and lighthearted words that tumble from an overflowing spirit. But that is not necessarily so. Psalm 65:1 describes a different kind of praise: "Praise awaits you, O God, in Zion; to you our vows will be fulfilled."

I've been told that the Hebrew word for *awaiting* means "quiet trust." Those words don't sparkle with effervescence. It's like saying, "I have prayed about this burden, and now, Lord, I will quietly wait on You even before I see the answer. I expect it. And this is my sacrifice of praise to You—I believe and trust."

Please remember this: Most of the verses written about praise in God's Word were voiced by people who were faced with crushing heartaches, injustice, treachery, slander, and scores of other difficult situations. They knew that the sacrifice of praise was a key to victory on their spiritual journey.

FIXING MY HEART ON PRAISE

I remember a time when I was asked—almost forced—to present a sacrifice of praise to God. During the years when I was first in the hospital, I struggled to put together two sensible words in prayer to God. I would lie in bed and dream of the day the pain would go away. As well-intentioned as my nurses were, their starched white uniforms and name tags only added to the institutional feeling of that place. I hated my life.

A Place of Sacrifice

I gave up on prayer. Praise? Far be it from me. I found solace in the luxury of a complaining tongue. I savored my anger, my resentment. I simply could not understand how a good God could allow something like my accident to happen to one of His children.

My good friend, Steve Estes, began to set me straight. I liked this young Christian man because he always brought me Dunkin' Donuts or pizza or RC colas. So whenever he opened his Bible, I listened. Then came the day when he read 1 Thessalonians 5:18, "Give thanks in all circumstances, for this is God's will for you in Christ Jesus."

He closed his Bible, looked at me and said gently, "Joni, it's about time you got around to giving thanks in that wheelchair of yours."

"I can't do that," I said, a little shocked. "It wouldn't be spontaneous. I don't feel it, and I'm not going to be a hypocrite. I was enough of a hypocrite when I was in high school. I don't want to be a hypocrite anymore. I'm not going to give thanks when I don't feel like it."

Steve said, "Wait a minute, Joni, read the verse again. It doesn't say you have to feel like a million bucks in everything. It says, 'Give thanks in all circumstances, for this is God's will for you in Christ Jesus.' Your thanks may not be spontaneous, but it can be a sacrifice. Trusting God's will is not necessarily having trusting feelings."

I argued, "I just can't thank God when I don't know why all this is happening."

Steve chided me gently. "Joni, even if the Lord were to tell you all the reasons why, it would be more than you could understand. God's ways are past finding out. You're just at the starting block of this long journey of life in a wheelchair. Don't expect to understand all the ins and outs from the very beginning."

"But I don't *feel* thankful," I whined.

"Well, the verse doesn't say 'feel thankful'—it says, 'give thanks.' There's a big difference."

So I gritted my teeth and, through tears, gave thanks for where I was at in life.

"Okay, Lord, I thank You for this hospital bed. I would really rather have the pizza and Dunkin' Donuts, but if You want me to have cafeteria oatmeal tomorrow, that's fine. And Lord, I thank You that physical therapy is benefiting me—thank You for all the flat-on-my-back ballet routines. Lord, I'm grateful that when I practiced writing the alphabet today with that pencil between my teeth, it didn't look like chicken scratch."

Some time later, I changed. Thankful feelings began to well up. It was as though God rewarded me with the feeling of gratitude for having obeyed and "given thanks."

And when I began to see that through giving thanks God was changing me and making me more like Jesus, it was no longer an effort to express gratitude. Perhaps in the beginning it had cost me my logic and my complaining, but praise came more easily after I saw the effects of such a sacrifice.

WHAT MAKES PRAISE COSTLY

I can hear someone saying, "That's fine, Joni, but I'm not you. I handle problems differently. I put up with my hardships because they're my lot in life. I simply take a deep breath, and God and I charge ahead."

Now if I've described you, then you're the type who feels

resigned to life. You may have a bit of the stoic in you, occasionally feeling like a martyr. But be honest—is resigning yourself to your problems really offering a sacrifice? I think you'll agree: Resignation is *not* a sacrifice of praise.

Then there are those folks who submit to their problems. They "ho" and they "hum" and sigh heavily. These dear people make certain everybody around sees they are bearing an impossible burden. But submission is not a sacrifice of praise either.

Well then, just what makes up a sacrifice of praise?

First, please don't think that you must be perfect in your praises to the Lord. Remember, He is not a rigid, unyielding God who forgets that "we are dust"; He "knows how we are formed" and remembers that we are only human (Psalms 103:14; 78:39). No matter how small or great the sacrifice, God knows the motive of your heart when you offer Him praise.

I learned that lesson in an odd way a few years ago.

You see, in the eighties, before the political changes in Poland, Ken and I visited that country where we spoke in churches and toured rehabilitation centers. When I returned to the States, I tried to share my impressions of Eastern Europe with a friend. I wanted to describe the warm and wonderful memory of being hugged by dear old Polish women who smelled faintly and sweetly of garlic. The hint of garlic was on their sweaters, coats, hands, even on their breath. Maybe before, garlic would have turned my nose, but since my visit, garlic became synonymous with laughter and smiles, happy embraces with new friends. Garlic meant…Poland.

But as I was about to describe this memory, I stopped short. You see, I don't think I could have explained that garlic equaled good things. To those of us in the West, garlic does not evoke the impression of a sweet, fragrant aroma. (Well, maybe it does if we're scarfing down our grandmother's famous lasagna.) For the most part, in this country the smell of garlic is about as pleasant as skunk spray.

One person's fragrance is another person's dread.

I occasionally think about that when I offer my sacrifices of praise to God. I want my offerings to be "a sweet-smelling aroma, an acceptable sacrifice, well pleasing to God" (Philippians 4:18, NKJV). I know what's on my heart as I wrench words of praise out of pain or hardship, and I believe God knows what's on my heart as well: "God, I'm hurting but You're my help...(long pause)...and I praise You...(brief moment of doubt, then a quick recovery)... and I will trust You...(am I sure? Yes, I am)...and rest in You (another long pause)...in Jesus' name, Amen."

That may not sound like a sacrifice of praise to some, and if certain people were listening in, they'd think my sacrifice of praise smelled like garlic. They'd turn up their nose; they just wouldn't understand. But I know...God knows. And that's all that counts.

To summarize, when I think of a sacrifice of praise, I think of the word *embrace*. Embracing the will of God, even when the feelings aren't there, is offering to God your heart, wholly dedicated to His purpose. It is believing that, according to Romans 12, you can prove in practice that God's will for you is good and acceptable and perfect.

It'll cost—but oh, the worth of those words you offer your Lord.

IF YOU CAN PRAISE GOD IN THIS...

You hear mothers say it all the time.

Their kids want to stay home, complaining of cramps or a headache, but as soon as the school bus leaves the corner, they bound out of bed, pull the games off the shelf, flip on the TV, or run downstairs to raid the fridge.

And what do moms all over the country say?

"If you're well enough to do that, then you're well enough to go to school."

I heard a similar line while dieting a few months ago. At a friend's house, I turned down a luscious-looking piece of walnut cake topped with whipped cream icing, sprinkled with nuts.

My friend regarded me for a moment. "If you can turn down *this*," she said, "then you can turn down anything!"

You can almost hear God say the same thing to us. "If you can praise and glorify Me in *this* circumstance, My child, you can glorify Me in anything." And it's true...

...as we wade through crushing disappointments

...or battle confusing family problems

...or grit our teeth and learn contentment in the middle of a painful illness

...or tearfully accept the sudden loss of a loved one.

We might at first think it curious that God so often uses suffering to make our lives "to the praise of His glory," as it says in Ephesians. I mean, aren't there better ways we can glorify God—or at least easier ones?

Yes, it is curious—and frequently beyond our understanding. But the truth remains...whenever a Christian is found faithful in affliction, repaying good for evil, returning love for abuse, holding steadfast through suffering, or loving in the middle of loneliness or grief, or embracing a place of sacrifice…the Lord receives the truest, brightest, most radiant kind of glory possible.

And if we can be found glorifying Him in that manner, God will open up all kinds of new opportunities, new circumstances in which to glorify Him. He'll do so because He knows we can be trusted, we can handle it with grace.

Maybe right now you're at a place in your life where you just can't see praise to God issuing forth from your response to trials. The dishes are piling up, your friend continues to misunderstand you, you haven't had a restful weekend in a month of Sundays, and your painful arthritis just won't be eased.

Let me tell you something. If you can glorify God through a patient response right now—in the middle of these things—then you can glorify God *anywhere.*

A LIVING SACRIFICE

I don't think we can talk about the sacrifice of praise without considering the bigger picture: our living sacrifice. We are to offer our bodies "as living sacrifices, holy and pleasing to God— this is your spiritual act of worship" (Romans 12:1).

A living sacrifice. I used to think of a bloody oblation on top of a brazen altar. Yuck. Well, that Old Testament image may not be all that different from what Paul meant in Romans 12. Frankly, when I read that verse I see myself on an altar. But this is where it changes—as soon as God strikes the match to light the flame of some fiery trial in my life, I imagine myself doing what any living sacrifice might do: I crawl off the altar!

This, to put it simply, is the dilemma Christians face. Living offerings have a way of creeping off the altar when the flames of a frustrating ordeal get a bit too hot. But the theme resounds through Scripture: He who loses his life for Christ's sake shall find it. Take up your cross—your altar of sacrifice—and follow Jesus. Since we died with Christ, we shall live with Him. If we die with Him, we shall reign with Him. There are scores of verses which sound the same theme.

As demanding as it may seem, God says that we are to present our bodies as living sacrifices, for this is our *reasonable* service. What's more, while we're on the altar, we're to praise God for the trial, because He is using it to mold us into the image of His Son. As our bodies are living sacrifices, our lips offer the sacrifice of praise. Sound reasonable?

Humanly speaking, no. With God's grace, yes.

Have you caught yourself crawling off the altar lately? Do you say you trust God with a certain problem and then sneak off the Lord's table to take things into your own hands? Or do you bargain with God from the altar, suggesting He turn down the flame a bit, as though He needed advice? Or do you argue with God about the length of time He has got you in the hot seat?

There's no getting around it. In view of God's mercies, in view of His single and great oblation for us, He asks of you and me the only kind of spiritual worship that is holy and pleasing to Him. A living offering you must be. Yes, you may squirm under the heat of the trial, but that doesn't change God's command. He's urging you today to get back up on the altar. Let your life—your heart, your words, your body—be an offering of praise to God. And make a decision to accept and embrace the place of sacrifice in which you find yourself.

YOUR QUIET PLACE...

Pray as you sing this sacrifice of praise!

Take my life and let it be
Consecrated, Lord, to Thee;
Take my moments and my days;
Let them flow in ceaseless praise,
Let them flow in ceaseless praise.

Take my hands and let them move
At the impulse of Thy love;
Take my feet and let them be
Swift and beautiful for Thee,
Swift and beautiful for Thee.

Take my will and make it Thine;
It shall be no longer mine;
Take my heart, it is Thine own;
It shall be Thy royal throne,
It shall be Thy royal throne.

Take my love, my Lord,
I pour At Thy feet its treasure store;
Take myself and I will be
Ever, only, all for Thee,
Ever, only, all for Thee.

A Place of Sacrifice

CHAPTER FIFTEEN

A PLACE OF VICTORY

O, do not pray for easy lives.
Pray to be stronger men.
Do not pray for tasks equal to your powers.
Pray for powers equal to your tasks.

Phillip Brooks, *Going Up to Jerusalem*

Words of praise. Do we really understand their power? Do we grasp the mighty force behind the things we say? Do we recognize the dynamics behind the sentences we speak to each other? The things we say before God? Before the Devil? No wonder the tongue is given so much attention in the book of James!

I had a friend whose life was a story of praise and victory. Denise was my roommate for almost two years when I was in the hospital. She was blind and paralyzed, a beautiful seventeen-year-old black high school girl from Baltimore. I had the advantage of being able to sit up in a wheelchair once in a while, but Denise remained in bed.

Denise's bed was catty-corner to mine, which was tucked up against a window. She had no window, but being blind, I'm

PLACE:
The Girl's Ward,
State Rehab Institute
Maryland

TIME:
November 1968

not sure it would have meant much. Being paralyzed, she couldn't hold a book or reach for the knobs on a bedside TV set. And as for conversation, it took real effort for her to murmur even a few sentences. Friends did occasionally drop by, but a prolonged stay in the hospital eventually weeds out all but the most committed visitors. In the end, it was mainly her mom, a wonderful Christian, who faithfully took the crosstown bus on Friday nights to sit at the bedside of her dying daughter. From my bed, I could hear her low voice, praying with Denise, reading Scripture. Sweet slivers of psalms and pieces of proverbs would drift through the atmosphere of that crazy place...like little shafts of light piercing dark clouds.

I pretended not to hear, riveting my attention to *I Spy*, or *Laugh In*, or whatever was on the tube. I resented Denise and her mom, because I was so bitterly angry. But as the months wore on, I found myself glad for the company of that gentle, soft-spoken girl. Her presence—quiet at as she was—eased the sharp loneliness.

The amazing thing about Denise was that she never complained. The room often smelled sour from hospital odors. The sheets were dirty. The nurses, overworked and underpaid, were often gruff. Somebody it seemed was always playing a radio too loud in the nurse's station opposite our ward. And, at least to me, it was depressing that the high point of everyone else's afternoon seemed to be the soap operas which blared out of the room next door.

I remember once asking a nurse, "What time is it, please."

She answered, "Why? You *goin'* somewhere, honey?"

It really hurt. "No...no, I guess I'm not going anywhere at all, but—could I please know the time?"

A Quiet Place in a Crazy World

What an awful place it was. Yet Denise was such a lesson to me. I came from white, middle-class suburbia. Gracious, well-kept homes. Sweet-smelling, green-lawned, oak-treed avenues. Denise's life had been much different, with so few of those advantages.

She didn't trash talk like the other girls. And even though she was dying, her mouth was full of prayers and thanksgiving.

I'll never forget that praise. Looking back, I've become convinced that our hospital room was cleansed of demons and dark spirits of resentment, anger, lust, and self-destruction by her sweet sacrifice of praise. And I can't help wondering if God began His work of emotional redemption in my life through Denise, who, blind and paralyzed, paved the way, gaining the victory over the Devil in our room.

In Ephesians 3:10 we read, "His intent was that now, through the church, the manifold wisdom of God should be made known to the rulers and authorities in the heavenly realms." In other words, Denise, lying in her bed, may not have been much of a testimony to the busy doctors and nurses or to occasional friends who dropped by, but her praise to God reached far beyond that hospital room to touch the heavenlies.

Denise, in praising the Lord, was winning a battle that you and I only glimpse now and then. She was living on a higher plane, a dimension that I wasn't sure even existed. Denise's life was the battleground upon which the mightiest forces of the universe converged in warfare. And she gained the victory through her praise to God.

OUR WATCHFUL WITNESSES

You and I are hardly in Denise's condition. In fact, unlike Denise, you may rub shoulders with scores of people every day.

A Place of Victory

Your testimony is seen by hundreds of people in a week—the bag boy at the local supermarket, the gas station attendant who fills your tank, the woman at the dry cleaners, your neighbor, the people at PTA, your friends at choir rehearsal. You meet people every day. Do they see in you a life devoted to godly praise?

And even if you're living alone in a small apartment, hardly interacting with anyone, your commitment to praise God counts. For there are a great many "somebodies" watching you. God uses your praise as a witness to angels and demons about His wisdom and power. When you bite your tongue from the luxury of complaining, you are gaining victory against the Devil. When you praise God, you are showing the heavenly hosts, powers, and principalities, the demons of darkness, and the angels of light that your great God is worthy of praise—no matter what your circumstances.

Our words of praise reach farther than we can imagine. Victory is found in praise. The outer realms of darkness shudder with the repercussions of our praise, and our words of adoration to the Lord have a rippling effect throughout all of heaven and hell. Devils scatter and strongholds are shattered.

PRAISE LIFTS BURDENS

Do you remember those high school chemistry days when your class fooled around—excuse me, *experimented*—with litmus paper? Remember, it was that little strip of paper that you would place in certain liquids to see if they were acid or alkaline. I can't remember what color the litmus paper turned if you dipped it in to acid—I think it was blue. And it turned red if the substance was alkaline.

I thought it was rather amazing when, with a tight grip, I

would hold a piece of litmus paper, open my palm, and the paper had turned red. A friend squeezed another piece of litmus, and his turned blue. Somebody else's litmus didn't turn any color at all. We laughed at the guy who was the most acidic of us, telling him he was an old sourpuss.

Since I've married, I've realized that silly high school game with litmus paper can tell a lot about a person. Sometimes I think God intends my husband Ken to be, well, a big piece of litmus paper. And in marriage where two people can't help but be pressed up against one another, Ken has a way of revealing who I am and what I'm made of deep inside.

For instance, I hate those times when I'm mad as a hornet and he stays cool as a cucumber. That's when he's like a piece of litmus paper. His patience and love only show up my own lovelessness and selfishness. The more love he demonstrates, the more ugly I feel in my own anger. I'm an old sourpuss up against him.

To be fair, there are plenty of moments when he is upset over some silliness and God gives me the grace to demonstrate love. That's when I'm like a piece of litmus paper to Ken. The sweeter I am, the more convicted he becomes.

Not long ago Ken and I had one of those "litmus test" quarrels. I found him using my good eyebrow tweezers to pick fleas off Scruffy, our dog. I couldn't believe it. He didn't even ask—he just rummaged around in my bathroom drawer, pulled out my tweezers, and proceeded to pick fleas off the dog. Then he didn't even wipe the tweezers with Lysol. He just dropped them back in my drawer.

I was outraged! "What in the world are you doing?"

That was all it took for him to remind me that I ought to

tell the girls who get me up in the morning to quit using his razors to shave my underarms!

Before you know it, we were quarreling hot and heavy. The words flew back and forth, and after half an hour, Ken slammed the door on me in the bedroom. I was fuming, so I decided I would enjoy the tactical satisfaction of turning my wheelchair to the sliding glass door to stare out at the backyard. When he returned to the bedroom, he'd find me there and feel bad.

Twenty minutes went by, and finally Ken walked back in. He sighed, sat on the edge of the bed, and shook his head. We sat there in stubborn silence.

Finally I spoke up. "I'm sorry, Ken. I don't like you."

He thought and then retorted, "I don't like you either."

"What are we going to do?" I asked.

"I don't know."

Another long moment passed. "I guess we ought to pray."

"Okay, you start."

My eyes were shooting such pointed darts, I don't know how Ken could pray, but he clasped his fingers tightly and began mouthing well-worn phrases. His voice faltered and he stumbled with his words. He spoke about the goodness and greatness of the Lord, yet I knew his heart wasn't in it.

I resented the effort my husband was making. The more he talked about how great God was, the more loveless I felt. It was as though Ken's words were a piece of litmus paper. God was pressing his prayer up against me, and my pH balance looked sour, so full of acid.

I tried to close my ears to Ken's words of praise. Even though his prayer wasn't spontaneous, it was genuine. Conviction grew in me. Mysteriously, Ken's words became

A Quiet Place in a Crazy World

softer, and I began to hear his heart break in his prayer. Tears came to my eyes, and my anger dissipated—it was all I could do to keep from stopping Ken from praying so I could tell him how much I loved him.

I had never seen anything so beautiful as my husband sitting there praising God. He looked up with tears in his eyes and said, "Your turn."

I was numb. Finally I stammered, "Ken, I feel awful. I just need to confess to God how rotten I am. I can't believe I made such a big deal over a pair of eyebrow tweezers."

I bowed my heart before the Lord, and next thing I knew, my husband and I were singing praises to God together. After a few moments, Ken said, "Joni, I feel like a burden has just been lifted off my shoulders." I looked at my watch. "Did that feeling happen just five seconds ago?"

"Yes, it did."

"I don't believe it. That's exactly when I felt the same heavy load lift off me." The air was lighter. The room even seemed brighter. The burden was gone. We embraced, relieved that our praise had had turned a troublesome turmoil into victory. Praise had brought us closer together and our marriage took a giant step forward—all because God gave us victory through praise.

PRAISE IS OUR BEST WEAPON

Praising God was the last thing on our mind that day we started quarreling. In the middle of all that fighting, I would have sworn Ken was my enemy. But praise helped me see that my spouse was not the enemy. Nor were the circumstances.

The same is true for you. Your friends are not the adversary. Your children aren't, and neither is your boss at work. We wrestle not against the flesh and blood of daily problems—our enemy is Satan. Our battle is with him.

If you think you have it tough, consider the story of Paul and Silas told in Acts 16. These two preachers were falsely accused by the owners of a slave girl who had been freed from a demon. Upset that their means of financial support was now gone, they accused Paul and Silas of throwing the city into an uproar.

The magistrates ordered Paul and Silas to be stripped and beaten. After being flogged, they were put in chains and thrown into prison. The jailer placed them in the innermost dungeon and guarded them carefully.

Imagine their pain—their wounds were caked with dried blood; welts and bruises covered their backs; and the damp prison air went right through them. Perhaps Paul felt faint or Silas was sick to his stomach.

Who would have blamed them for whining or complaining? But Paul and Silas directed their thoughts toward God, not their accusers. They chose to pray and sing hymns loud enough for the other prisoners to hear—in other words, they triumphed in their praise.

Even though men and Satan attacked them, Paul and Silas won the battle *with their words*. Perhaps they even cried out the words of Psalm 106:47, "Save us, O LORD our God, and gather us from among the heathen, to give thanks unto thy holy name, and to triumph in thy praise" (KJV).

Once again, we win wars with our words. Victory comes as a result of praise.

Has it ever struck you that your praise teaches the hosts of heaven about God? That your prayers are a powerful testimony to both angels and demons? Amazing, isn't it?

The next time you're tempted to think that your response to your trials isn't doing anybody any good, before you give up the battle, turn to Ephesians 3:10. It might help to remind you that somebody's watching—and you might even find yourself listening for the rustling of wings. In fact, why don't you read Ephesians 3:10 right now:

> His intent was that now, through the church, the manifold wisdom of God should be made known to the rulers and authorities in the heavenly realms.

Spend a few moments in praise to God, mindful that others are listening!

CHAPTER SIXTEEN

A PLACE OF CONFIDENCE

I have been driven many times to my knees
by the overwhelming conviction
that I had nowhere else to go.

Abraham Lincoln

I was a little girl on a big horse, and all was right in God's good world. My horse clip-clopped lazily along the river trail. I lay on my stomach on her broad back, just a kid in bare feet and rolled up jeans on a warm summer morning. Reaching for an occasional willow branch, I'd let the leaves scrape off into my hand as we went by, pulling the limb further and further back and then letting it fling.

PLACE:
Gorsuch Switch Trail
along the
Patapsco River
TIME:
Summer 1962

Chewing on a long straw, I let the languid summer sounds drift down on me…the birds in the woods…the crickets in the rocks…the liquid murmur of the river…a soft wind sighing in the willows. Rounding a bend in the trail, I paused to wave at three fishermen on the opposite bank. The cool river smells blended with the fragrance of ripe, new-mown hay from the Cauthorn's field.

167

I climbed down and sat on the bank, watching the green water glide by. My horse cropped sweet grass, pausing to snort now and then shake the flies from her head. I actually sat between her front legs, hanging on to one of her shins, resting my head against her velvet knee.

A deep feeling of satisfaction and pleasure filled me. God was in his heaven, taking care of my horse and me. I had not professed Christ at that point in my life, but I was a child of deep spirituality, and I thanked Him with the simple gratitude of a child.

He had given me summer and freedom and a happy family and a big gentle horse for a companion.

Somehow I knew…I would know this God better. My confidence began to grow.

★ ★ ★

A few years later, my love of horses took a more serious turn.

I began training horses to jump and would often enter them in horse shows around Maryland and Pennsylvania. I'd polish my boots, soap my saddle, and starch and iron my shirt. I worked hard but nowhere near as hard as my thoroughbred, Auggie.

My horse was one of those tall, thin thoroughbreds with long legs. He looked like an adolescent who hadn't grown into his feet yet. Auggie didn't have the best conformation, but those legs carried us over some of the highest and broadest fences. And in the show ring, he was absolutely trusting and obedient to me.

When we would approach the first fence, I'd simply tighten my knees against the saddle, and off he would go in a flash.

He'd confidently canter toward the fence; I'd angle his head, and he'd fly swiftly over it. I'd rein his head toward the next fence, and he'd leap over that one, hurdling a complex maze of jumps.

Maneuvering a horse through a confusing series of difficult hurdles requires a trusting and obedient horse. The horse has to trust that the rider knows what he's doing—I had knowledge of what lay ahead in the course and Auggie didn't. Trusting and obeying. Leading and guiding. Auggie and I lived our relationship in a place of confidence.

ARE YOU FACING HURDLES?

For us humans, the path of life before us often seems like an incredibly complex maze of hurdles we're expected to cross over. Have you ever felt like you were on a track, running with all your might and not knowing what was to come next? We can't see over the hurdle, and because it's so high, we're not sure we want to even go on to the next one. We feel like disobeying. We feel like running out on the course of life.

But listen. Auggie's trusting response did not hinge on his approval of the course. My horse didn't understand jumps. He had no idea about the degree of difficulty. All he knew was me.

I wish I were more like my horse! Isaiah 1:3 says, "The ox knows his master, the donkey his owner's manger, but Israel does not know, my people do not understand." Why is it we cannot, do not, trust God? Maybe we just don't know who God is, or how much He has done for us.

Look at Paul's confidence in the Lord. In Scripture we never hear Paul say, "I understand why these things are happening, Lord, and so I'll offer you praise." No. His praise was often a sacrifice because he *didn't* know what was around the next

A Place of Confidence

bend. Nevertheless, Paul trusted and obeyed. He didn't know why things were happening, what was ahead, or how difficult it would be, but he knew in Whom he believed: "Yet I am not ashamed, because I know whom I have believed, and am convinced that he is able to guard what I have entrusted to him for that day" (2 Timothy 1:12).

For Paul, the supreme reason he could praise God was simply this: he knew Jesus. The apostle was able to praise the Lord because Jesus had purchased his trust at the cross.

And Jesus has proved Himself worthy of your confidence, too.

WHEN YOU CAN'T SEE OVER THE HURDLE

Nothing beats good advice. A man named Ted Smith wrote to me a few years ago and offered this: "Many believers gaze at their problems and glance at the Lord. But I tell you to gaze at the Lord and glance at your problems."

Great advice! Too many of us fix our eyes on our problems—the hurdles—and we start measuring the height of the next jump. In so doing, we glance occasionally at the Lord only to make sure He's aware of all the hardships these hurdles are causing us.

Trouble is, the course God has set before us seems so...difficult! The dog has tracked Alpo all over the kitchen floor. Your husband has called to say he'll be late. The saucepans are boiling over, and the burning casserole is staining your oven. Teenagers are wrestling in the bedroom above your kitchen. Little wonder you stand there with the dish towel in your hand, droop-shouldered and dumbfounded, not knowing what to do.

You mutter an obligatory prayer as you tramp upstairs to

referee the latest family argument. Sound familiar? You sigh in frustration as God barely gets noticed in all the hoopla.

What we need here is more than a prayer mumbled in obligation. We need the attitude of Abraham Lincoln when he said, "I have been driven many times to my knees by the overwhelming conviction that I had nowhere else to go." We need a different focus.

Consider Hebrews 12:2-3:

> Let us fix our eyes on Jesus, the author and perfecter of our faith, who for the joy set before him endured the cross, scorning its shame, and sat down at the right hand of the throne of God. Consider him who endured such opposition from sinful men, so that you will not grow weary and lose heart.

It really is a matter of focus, isn't it? Consider Jesus. He had one heavy cross to bear, but He fixed His sight on the joy before Him. And we are to do the same.

So what about the burning casserole, the dirty kitchen floor, and the screaming kids upstairs? They haven't changed. But your focus has. Don't gaze at your problems while you only glance at the Lord. Get life in focus. Gaze at the Lord—be confident in Him—and your problems won't cause you to grow weary and lose heart.

EARNING THE PRIZE

Auggie, my wonderful horse, taught me a lot about why I ought to praise God. After the course in the show ring was completed, and he was hot and lathered, I'd jump down and lead him out to the paddock. Often the judges called us back into the ring. As we stood in front of the judges' box, Auggie would shake his head and stamp his feet impatiently until a person of great importance walked up to him—and handed me the trophy. Auggie did all the work, but I received the honors.

Do you see the parallel? You and I are in training to trust and obey. This whole adventure we're on is a growing relationship of trust and obedience between us and the One who is holding the reins in our life. While we are leaping through our complex maze of hurdles in this pattern of life, the eyes of the Judge are upon us. And on the day of completion, when we have been "trained" in godliness, the Lord Jesus will walk up to us and award us a prize. What an honor! The Bible makes it clear that you and I are to be for the praise of Christ's glory. Consider these verses from Ephesians:

> He predestined us to be adopted as his sons through Jesus Christ, in accordance with his pleasure and will.... In him we were also chosen, having been predestined according to the plan of him who works out everything in conformity with the purpose of his will.... I pray also that the eyes of your heart may be enlightened in order that you may know the hope to which he has called you, the riches of his glorious inheritance in the saints (Ephesians 1:5,11,18).

Do you see? We receive the inheritance of Christ so that we may bring Him glory! All the praise goes to the Lord Jesus. Sure, we do much of the work here on earth—there's a lot of training and preparation. The course is long and complex, and at times we get weary and wonder if it's really worth it all. But every moment the eyes of the Judge are upon us. He sees our successes and our failures. For all our efforts, for all the times we obey, Jesus will receive the glory.

As you go about your duties today, remember what—remember who—your work is for. It is to be for the praise of His glory. The more you obey, the greater the honor He receives.

Jesus gets the glory—there's no better reason to praise Him.

YOUR QUIET PLACE...

Try sharpening your focus right now. Spend a little time thinking about Hebrews 12:2-3:

> Let us fix our eyes on Jesus, the author and perfecter of our faith, who for the joy set before him endured the cross, scorning its shame, and sat down at the right hand of the throne of God. Consider him who endured such opposition from sinful men, so that you will not grow weary and lose heart.

Perhaps you can write this out and tape it above your kitchen sink, on the dash of your car, or above your desk. That way, life will stay in focus.

Something that helps me keep my life in focus is the doxology, the church's anthem of victorious praise. If you know the tune, sing it now:

Praise God from Whom all blessings flow,

Praise Him, all creatures here below.

Praise Him above, ye heavenly hosts,

Praise Father, Son, and Holy Ghost.

Keep this in mind next time you're facing life's challenges! Place Your confidence in One who cannot fail.

A Place of Confidence

CHAPTER SEVENTEEN

A PLACE OF GLORY

Prayer crowns God with the honor and glory due to His name, and God crowns prayer with assurance and comfort.

Thomas Benton Brooks

Sometimes I like to think that my prayers of praise are like one or two small drops in a vast ocean of joyful adorations that have gone up before God for countless ages. In other words, our lives of prayer aren't the only lives that touch the heart of God.

Ken and I arrived at St. Paul's on a Sunday afternoon, in time for the late service. He had quite a job drawing me and my chair up all those steps. Once inside, I wheeled slowly down the center aisle, my head tilted back to gape at the arched, gilded ceiling rising to a massive central dome. The dark wooden pews were worn down to the grain from decades of polishing.

PLACE:
St. Paul's Cathedral, London

TIME:
June 1988

As we sat in the hush of the cool cathedral, I was carried away by the voice of the great bells above me. The few of us gathered for the service bowed our heads in quiet respect as we prayed in this sanctuary where thousands of saints had worshiped for centuries. As in days of old, candles warmed the cathedral with a soft glow, reflecting off the faces of the boys in the choir. The choir chanted Gregorian canticles, an old and familiar harmony that has reached the rafters of that grand cathedral for hundreds of years. The great sanctuary was filled with flowers, their fragrance blending with the warm smell of sweet wax.

In St. Paul's, people prayed for safety during the sweep of the Black Plague. George Whitefield pled for the souls of his countrymen. Perhaps David Livingstone sought God's blessing there before embarking on his missionary journeys. Kings and queens of Europe bowed their knees in prayer in St. Paul's; dignitaries and statesmen, too. Very possibly, the Pilgrims and settlers who sailed from England to America had friends who prayed for their safety from under the arches where I was sitting.

As I stared at the high-gilded ceiling, the heavy tapestries, and the carved marble statues, I was reminded of Hebrews 12:1: "Therefore, since we are surrounded by such a great cloud of witnesses, let us throw off everything that hinders and the sin that so easily entangles, and let us run with perseverance the race marked out for us."

Wheeling away after the service, I thought of all the praying Christians who now sit in the grandstands of heaven. They have set an example, and God has used their prayers to protect His Word, advance His gospel, strengthen His church, and teach us today of the power of praise and prayer.

But "grandstand people" don't have to be saints of old. These heroes of the faith can be our neighbors, our pastors—

even you can be a spiritual hero. You can be a grandstand person to someone else who is waiting to see another Christian persevere in prayer, take seriously the call to intercede, and believe mightily that praise has power.

Compared to Notre Dame, St. Paul's Cathedral is just a shiny new church on the corner. Ken and I stood at a little distance to fill our eyes with the visage of this hoary, medieval giant. Its towers, darkened by long centuries of smoke and soiled air, soared into the seamless blue of a spring Parisian sky.

PLACE:
Notre Dame Cathedral, Paris

TIME:
May 1993

I asked Ken to park me beside the statue of a mounted Charlemagne, while he walked about looking for camera angles, snapping away with his Nikon.

A dark woman with a scarf over her head sold lavender from a cart nearby. A few hundred yards away, a small crowd gathered to watch the antics of a mime troupe. Bathed in afternoon sunlight, the apple trees along the gently flowing Seine were mantled with pink-white blossoms.

Turning my eyes back to the ancient cathedral, I thought of how glorious the church of Christ is to stand throughout all of history. For well over a thousand years, the cathedral had been a silent witness to plagues, intrigues, the bloody French Revolution, and the bombings of Hitler. The cathedral watched, unmoved, as the Renaissance and Age of Enlightenment came and went. Kingdoms rose and fell. Wars exploded and receded. Notre Dame was there when Napoleon met his Waterloo. Prior to World War I, frightened soldiers destined for the Front knelt in its cool depths, beseeching God for mercy

A Place of Glory

and protection. The stone figures of the martyrs of the church have looked down on peasants and kings, shopkeepers and presidents, simple farm maidens and jeweled aristocrats.

I was moved—stirred in my heart—just as I had been at St. Paul's on another spring day. It wasn't the building that impressed me as much as the thought that Christ's church *endures* as history winds its way toward a conclusion. The gates of hell have not prevailed against it. I am one small voice in a mighty choir that stretches through the ages. My song of praise blends with the voice of millions from every corner of the world, every nation, every century. The hymn of praise has been rising to God's glory through the long millennia, and you and I have only just joined in.

We are only the most recent threads in a long, beautiful tapestry, woven by a hand beyond time. Yet in His sight, each tiny stitch is a significant part of the whole. And each little thread is infinitely precious. Each minute design contributes to a transcendent glory.

GLORY CLOSE AT HAND

"Glory."

That's one of those lofty, in-the-clouds words, isn't it? Difficult to visualize. Hard to get in focus. The meaning is either so heavy we can't keep a grip on it—or so high above our heads that we can't reach it.

We hear people talk about God's grace, righteousness, redemption, and glory and we nod our heads. Sure, all of those things are important, but sometimes the meaning seems a little, well, *distant* from our daily lives. What does God's glory have to do with finishing a report for school, changing the oil in the car, or getting the laundry folded?

At one time I felt "glory" must mean some kind of cosmic brilliance or blinding light. Images of long-ago Bethlehem would play on the screen of my mind, with magnificent heavenly beings shouldering back the night and shouting out, "Glory to God in the highest!"

In recent days, however, I've learned that "glory" comes closer to home than that. Much closer.

Glory, I've learned, is what God is all about. His essential being. Whenever you talk about His character or attributes—such as holiness, love, compassion, justice, truth, or mercy—that's God's glory. And when He reveals Himself in any of those qualities, we say that He is "glorifying Himself."

In times past, He revealed those qualities in both places and people. He still does.

Not long ago I entered a friend's home and immediately sensed the glory of God. No, that impression was not based on some heebie-jeebie feeling or super-spiritual instinct. And it had nothing to do with several Christian plaques I spotted hanging in the hallway. Yet there was a peace and orderliness that pervaded that home. Joy and music hung in the air. Although the kids were normal, active youngsters, everyone's activities seemed to dovetail together, creating the impression that the home had direction, that the kids really cared about each other, that the parents put love into action.

We didn't even spend that much time "fellowshipping" in the usual sense of the word—talking about the Bible or praying together. Yet we laughed. And really heard each other. And opened our hearts like family members.

A Place of Glory

After dinner I left that home refreshed. It was a place where God's essential being was on display. His kindness, His love, His justice. It was a place of glory.

So how is it that you and I can glorify God? It happens every time we reveal His attributes in the course of our daily lives. Every time you share the good news of Christ with another. Every time you reflect patience in the middle of an upsetting or perplexing problem. Every time you smile from the heart or offer an encouraging word. Whenever those around you see God's character displayed in your attitudes and responses, you are displaying His glory.

So you see, God's glory isn't reserved for some great cathedral or shimmery heavenly vista. It can shine out clearly while you are changing a flat on the freeway...or counseling an angry co-worker...or lying in a hospital bed...or balancing two crying babies in a church nursery.

Exciting as all of this is, Paul has news that's even better still.

And we, who with unveiled faces all reflect the Lord's glory, are being transformed into his likeness with ever-increasing glory, which comes from the Lord, who is the Spirit (2 Corinthians 3:18).

The more we look to the Lord Jesus throughout the hours and days of our lives, Paul is saying, the more we begin to actually resemble Him! The more we time we invest praising His beautiful name, the more His beauty begins to permeate our lives.

A SWEET REMINDER OF JESUS

Our simple praise brings delight to the Lord of the universe. Can you imagine?

You and I can actually move the heart of an almighty, eternal God. Just read these verses and imagine the smile of God: "Here is my servant, whom I uphold, my chosen one in whom I delight" (Isaiah 42:1). And also, "The LORD will take delight in you.... As a bridegroom rejoices over his bride, so will your God rejoice over you" (Isaiah 62:4-5).

What a privilege it is to bring God joy! The following will help illustrate what I mean.

I love crisp, cold days when I can smell the smoke of a cherry-wood fire from a neighbor's chimney. Or I can stick my head out the back bedroom window, draw a deep breath, and almost taste the scent of pine from the little woods on the other side of the fence. I love the smell of fresh, damp laundry hanging outside on the line.

In fact, to this day, smelling Tide laundry detergent brings back vivid memories of my father's T-shirts and good times helping my mom fold sweet-smelling towels. Fragrances bring beautiful memories to mind. I'm sure that's why the perfume industry is a multimillion-dollar business. Perfume experts know a whiff of English Leather or a sniff of Chanel No. 5 can make us recall crystal clear, wonderful remembrances.

However, God's Word knew the power of perfume long before the chemists at Revlon. In 2 Corinthians 2:14 Paul wrote, "But thanks be to God, who always leads us in triumphal procession in Christ and through us spreads everywhere the fragrance of the knowledge of him."

That idea was borrowed from the ancient Roman parades of triumph. The apostle Paul compared himself, first, to one of the prisoners led in long chains behind the conqueror's chariot;

then, to a servant bearing incense; and lastly, to the incense itself that rose all along the procession of triumph.

Paul knew the power behind a sweet fragrance. It is as though he were saying, "I desire to live that I may perpetually remind God of the obedience, sacrifice, and devotion of the Lord Jesus. I want my words and deeds to bring to the mind of God those wonderful, similar memories of the earthly life of Jesus."

Isn't that a glorious thought? Your prayers, like all acts of service, rise like a sweet-smelling savor, a fragrant sacrifice that pleases God (Philippians 4:18). And that fragrance of your prayers is a reminder to the Father of the sweet-smelling sacrifice of the life of His Son (Ephesians 5:2). Your prayers make God smile.

TO GOD BE THE GLORY

Picture yourself now at that great Day yet to happen. "For we must all appear before the judgment seat of Christ, that each one may receive what is due him for the things done while in the body, whether good or bad" (2 Corinthians 5:10).

It is your turn. Jesus looks through the books, smiles at you and says, "Well done, good and faithful servant! You have been faithful with a few things; I will put you in charge of many things" (Matthew 25:21). He hands you a crown. Perhaps a few crowns: The crown that will last (1 Corinthians 9:25-27), the crown of rejoicing (1 Thessalonians 2:19-20), the crown of righteousness (2 Timothy 4:8), the crown of life (James 1:12), and the crown of glory (1 Peter 5:2-4).

You feel the heavy diadem; you hold it and run your fingers over it. You can't believe the crown is really in your hands. As you stand there, other saints gather around and kneel before the King of kings to lay their crowns at His feet (Revelation 4:4,10). What do you see yourself doing—tightly clutching your crown, or falling to your knees and presenting it with tears of joy to your great God and Savior?

That Day is coming soon. Why wait until eternity to know the Lord intimately? Why delay until the judgment seat of Christ to offer Him praise? You have an open invitation to enter the heart of God through prayer and praise today. Prayer is your point of contact with the Lord of the universe. Prayer is an investment in heavenly glories above—much like those crowns.

You can find a quiet place in this crazy world we live in. You can find a life-changing Refuge as you draw near to your God in prayer and praise. He hears you. He loves you. And He meets you in your place of need...wherever you are.

YOUR QUIET PLACE...

Always remember, you have the opportunity to communicate intimately and personally with the Son of God through prayer. But praying, just like any communication, is something you want to do with someone you know. If you don't know the Lord Jesus, you can meet Him right now with a very simple prayer like this one:

Dear Lord Jesus, I realize my life has been far from You, and I know that sin has been the barrier between us. Please come into my heart and mind and spirit, and Father, through Your forgiveness, make me the person You want me to be. Forgive me for turning away from You. Give me the power to follow You as I invite You to be the Lord of my life. Thank You for the difference You will make because of the Lord Jesus. Amen.

FOR GROUP DISCUSSION

CHAPTER 1: A PLACE OF SEEKING

1. What does it mean to seek God with all your heart and with all your soul? How would you explain this to a new believer?

2. How do you usually prepare your heart for prayer? What would you tell someone who wanted to know how to prepare his or her heart for prayer?

3. When is it difficult for you to pray with heartfelt honesty? What would help you be more honest with God?

4. What do you admire about Job's reaction to his time of crisis? What could you do to make your prayer more like his?

5. What are some of the barriers, events, feelings, or circumstances that prevent you from preparing your heart for prayer? What can you do to overcome them?

6. In what way has your journey through life been one of prayer and praise? What would you like to improve about your prayer and praise?

CHAPTER 2: A PLACE OF REFUGE

1. How was it that David could be so stunned by the greatness of the Lord's majesty (as in Psalm 8) and yet so drawn to the Lord as a safe, warm refuge?

2. As a child, what gave you a sense of security (blanket, stuffed animal, etc.)? What gives you security now?

3. What possible future crises could undermine your security and cause you to panic?

4. How can prayer help you feel safe and secure?

5. In what situations do you often feel small and insignificant? How does prayer make you feel small and important at the same time?

6. When do you need a refuge, a place that protects you and makes you feel safe?

7. How is God your refuge? How does prayer place you in God's safe house?

CHAPTER 3: A PLACE OF AWE

1. God is our Father...but He is also King of the Universe. What kind of balance ought those two thoughts bring to the way we approach Him in prayer?

2. What are some examples of careless habitual prayers? In what other ways are we too casual in our relationship with God?

3. What does it mean to be properly terrified before the Lord? Why is prayer serious business?

4. How have your prayers changed as you've grown in your faith?

5. How can you approach God with confidence as well as reverence?

6. What will help you remember to pray with reverence?

CHAPTER 4: A PLACE OF DUST AND ASHES

1. What guilty feelings sometimes stop you from praying?

2. When have you been afraid to pray? What were you afraid of?

3. What have you done to overcome barriers to prayer?

4. What does it mean for you to humble yourself when you pray? How does a humble attitude help you when you pray?

5. What attributes of God help you maintain a humble attitude in prayer?

A Quiet Place in a Crazy World

6. How would you pray differently if you were truly humble before God?

CHAPTER 5: A PLACE OF ASKING

1. What specific answers to prayer are impressed on your memory? What specific answers to prayer have you received recently?

2. What general prayers that you usually pray could you make more specific? When might prayers be *too* specific?

3. What does it mean to "wrestle with God" in prayer? What benefits come from persisting in prayer?

4. When have you wrestled with God in prayer? How did God change you in the process? How did God answer your prayer?

CHAPTER 6: A PLACE OF DISCIPLINE

1. Identify several "small disciplines" in your personal prayer life that could lead to larger, more significant disciplines?

2. In what ways is prayer like art and music?

3. What hard work is involved in praying? What must you practice?

4. From what you've read so far, what is a prayer warrior? What keeps you from being a prayer warrior?

5. What would you have to do to become more disciplined in praying?

CHAPTER 7: A PLACE OF LISTENING

1. Read again the poignant story of young Samuel at the Tent of Meeting (1 Samuel 3). What do you learn from this story about "listening to God"?

2. Identify the times in one of your normal days (if there is such a thing!) when you would regularly "shift gears" from one activity to another. How could listening to God become part of that activity shifting process?

For Group Discussion

4. What resources might help you to refocus on the Lord and begin to hear His voice?

5. What is the importance of *immediately* responding to the Lord's still small voice the moment we become aware of His speaking?

CHAPTER 8: A PLACE TO PLEAD YOUR CASE

1. What's good and what's bad about arguments?

2. When do you feel like arguing with God? How can these arguments improve your prayer?

3. How are talking, conversing, arguing, and praying different from each other?

4. Why is it helpful to support your prayers with reasons?

5. How might stating reasons for your requests affect the way you pray?

CHAPTER 9: A PLACE OF TAKING HOLD

1. What attributes of God can you name off the top of your head?

2. Of all God's attributes, which ones do you depend on the most?

3. What is your favorite attribute of God? How does it fit into your prayer life?

4. How can remembering God's faithfulness help you during difficult circumstances?

5. How can God's attributes be used like a great battering ram in prayer?

6. What should you do to become bolder in prayer?

CHAPTER 10: A PLACE OF PROMISE

1. When did someone disappoint you because he or she did not keep a promise?

2. How do we know that God always keeps His promises?

3. How has God proven His faithfulness to you in the past?

How does knowing that God is faithful affect the way you pray and live?

4. What particular promise in the Bible has been especially meaningful to you? How has it helped you?

5. How should the fact that God always keeps His promises change the way you pray from now on?

CHAPTER 11: A PLACE OF WORDLESS LONGING

1. When was a time you were with someone who was hurting and you did not know what to say?

2. Why does it seem difficult to pour out your deepest feelings to God? Why is it difficult to pray when you don't know what to say?

3. How do loving parents feel when a child needs something and doesn't know how to tell them? How might this be similar to the way God listens to our hurts?

4. Knowing that God hears us and understands us when we have no words, how should we pray?

5. How might you be able to share your feelings with God when you can't put them into words?

CHAPTER 12: A PLACE OF JESUS' NAME

1. When have you prayed one way only to find God answered some other way?

2. Have you ever prayed for healing with sincere and certain faith but nothing happened? What answer do you think you really received?

3. How could suffering and disappointment be one way God answers prayer?

4. What does fullness of joy mean to you? When have you experienced pure joy? How is joy different from peace or happiness?

5. How can you pray in a way consistent with Jesus' character and life?

For Group Discussion

6. What does praying in Jesus' name really mean to you?

CHAPTER 13: A PLACE OF PRAISE

1. In what ways is praise even more powerful when it arises out of life situations that are dark and distressing?
2. What is genuine praise?
3. For what can you praise God?
4. What word best describes each person of the Trinity?
5. Brag about someone you love. Then do the same with Jesus.
6. What does this chapter teach you about praising God?

CHAPTER 14: A PLACE OF SACRIFICE

1. What is sacrificial about praising God when you don't feel like it?
2. How would you describe the difference between praising God out of joy and blessing and praising Him out of sorrow and pain?
3. What's the difference between praising God *in* a bad situation, and thanking Him *for* a bad situation?
4. How does praise help us get through difficult problems?
5. What bothers you about being a living sacrifice? What thoughts give you peace about it?

CHAPTER 15: A PLACE OF VICTORY

1. Think of a friend who has a close relationship with God. What have you noted or learned about prayer from that person?
2. When would it be appropriate to praise God in the middle of a conflict, and when would it be inappropriate?
3. In what ways is praise like a weapon? Against whom is the weapon to be used?
4. How does praise help us succeed in living the Christian life?

5. What's the relationship between praise and confession?

6. For what can you praise God right now?

CHAPTER 16: A PLACE OF CONFIDENCE

1. What was one of your favorite childhood activities that you worked or practiced hard at (soccer, piano, dance, raising an animal, chess, swimming, etc.)? What insights, if any, does this give you into prayer?

2. When have you faced a hurdle in life that you couldn't see over?

3. What is often the worst time of your day or week? What could you do to focus on Christ at that time—gaze instead of glance at Him—that would help you get through it?

4. What are the biggest everyday hurdles you face? How can you focus your thoughts on Jesus as you approach them?

5. What can you do to change your focus?

CHAPTER 17: A PLACE OF GLORY

1. In your Christian walk so far, what's one worship experience that stands out? Where was it and why was it memorable?

2. When you think of someone "watching you from the grandstands," who comes to mind (both living and dead)? How does this motivate you?

3. Imagine finally seeing God face-to-face. What is the first thing that you would like to say or do? How can you do that now?

4. How has this book helped you find "a quiet place" in a sometime-crazy world?

ABOUT THE AUTHOR

Other books by Joni Eareckson Tada:

Joni, 1976, Zondervan Publishing House
A Step Further, 1978, Zondervan Publishing House
All God's Children, 1981, Zondervan Publishing House
Choices...Changes, 1986, Zondervan Publishing House
Friendship Unlimited, 1987, Harold Shaw Publishers
Secret Strength, 1988, Multnomah Press
Glorious Intruder, 1989, Multnomah Press
A Christmas Longing, 1990, Multnomah Press
When Is It Right to Die?, 1992, Zondervan Publishing House
Diamonds in the Dust, 1993, Zondervan Publishing House

Children's books:

Darcy, 1988, David C. Cook Publishing Co.
Darcy and the Meanest Teacher in the World, David C. Cook Publishing Co.

Darcy's Dog Dilemma, David C. Cook Publishing Co.
Jeremy, Barnabas, & the Wonderful Dream, 1987, David
C. Cook Publishing Co.
Meet My Friends, 1987, David C. Cook Publishing Co.
Ryan and the Circus Wheels, 1988, David C. Cook
Publishing Co.
The Great Alphabet Fight (with Steve Jensen), 1993,
Questar Publishers

Joni Eareckson Tada is founder and president of JAF
Ministries, a Christian organization that links the church with
disabled people through evangelism, encouragement, and edu-
cation.

If you or someone you know might benefit from the ministry
of JAF Ministries, you may write Joni at:
    JAF Ministries
    P.O. Box 3333
    Agoura Hills, CA 91301